AF225111

Three
Hearts

Three Hearts

An Anthology of Cephalopod Poetry

Edited by Sierra Nelson

World Enough Writers

Published in the United States of America by World Enough Writers

ISBN: 978-1-937797-56-0

Cover art: Jen Strongin jenstronginphotography.com

Endpapers: Britta Johnson thekmpi.net

Editor Photo by Leanne Dunic leannedunic.com

Designed by Tonya Namura using Gentium Basic and Harabara Hand.

This book was made possible thanks to time at Friday Harbor Labs, the Whiteley Center, and Mineral School.

For information, please contact the publisher:

World Enough Writers
c/o Concrete Wolf
PO Box 2220
Newport, OR 97365-0163

Email: WorldEnoughWriters@gmail.com

Website: https://worldenoughwriters.com

*For all who appreciate the brilliant variations
of life on Earth.*

*With special thanks to the Cephalopods and
Cephalopod Appreciators.*

*May we continue to grow in our
understanding of one another.*

"Most of our modern cephalopods have done away with this shell nonsense to some extent or another. Cuttlefish still have a chambered organ to control their buoyancy, but they hide it away inside, squid don't even use their remnant to float anymore, and octopus don't even have that. Squishiness abounds. Which is amazing in and of itself! In addition to their amazing (at times downright psychedelic) color changing abilities, many cephalopods can also actively change the texture and shape of their skin."

"And yet, for all their alien characteristics, there's something so personable about cephalopods. The cranky octopus, camouflage cover blown, suddenly appearing and swimming off in a YouTube video. Stories of clever octopus escape-artists touring aquaria after hours looking for a snack. Flamboyant cuttlefish sauntering about on pseudo-limbs showing off their bright colors and fancy patterns. For all our differences, for better or worse, cephalopods hold a mirror to humanity."
—Stephanie Crofts, PhD, from Away with the Shells

"Humans tend to think of themselves as the pinnacle of evolution, yet we have no construct to imagine the experience of developing a brain to control the brain we've got, much less eight that are controlling individual appendages. What would we do with such a highly developed brain? End world hunger and strife? Depart for distant worlds in the universe? Destroy ourselves even quicker than we are now? I am both enthralled and frightened by the idea. Before I go, I am told that if there are aliens living among us, it is the cephalopods. I, for one, agree."
—Derek Smith, PhD, from I, Octopus

CONTENTS

EDITOR'S NOTE

To Unfurl in Every Direction

Once at the Scripps Birch Aquarium in San Diego I spent a long while looking at a cuttlefish in a tank who also appeared to be curious about me. After a bit of mutual regard, the cuttlefish flashed a dark circle around their eyes, seeming to mimic my black eyeglasses. Was this a way to say, "I see you too"? Or were they asking me what *I* meant, an accidental stumbler into their language of color, my spectacles mistaken for clumsy chromatophores?

The idea behind this anthology emerges from that same sense of amazement sparked by interspecies connection, and a curiosity about how we as humans see and are seen through our interest in cephalopods.

The more we learn about cephalopods—octopus, squid, cuttlefish, chambered nautilus, and the now extinct ammonites and nautiloids—the more we both recognize them as kin and deepen our wonder at this alien *Other*. As fellow intelligent beings on planet Earth, we've learned that they, like us, also play, create, solve problems, remember, hold grudges, have favorites, play tricks, have personalities, plan great escapes, communicate complexly, express themselves with color and movement, make love, are devoted mothers, and even dream. Yet with their entirely different physiologies, this group of thinking "head-foot" invertebrates in the phylum Mollusca have also long evoked for humans what is strange, mysterious, or sometimes even monstrous: giant squids and krakens lurking in the ocean and abyss of our psyches. Sometimes it is the cephalopod's perceived Otherness for which we feel the most affinity: to love a cephalopod can be to love the parts of ourselves that have felt the most marginalized, ostracized, or misunderstood. And to understand a cephalopod is an invitation to stretch our sensory imagination: to consider what it means to have three hearts, or nine brains, to camouflage perfectly with our surroundings, or to disappear by glowing, to taste everything we touch.

This core-sample of contemporary, cephalopod-inspired writing reflects the variety of ways cephalopods intersect with our human lives and enter our creative inner worlds. The poems range in tone and style: heartbreaking, strange, reverent, funny, inspired by facts, steeped in the personal. Many of the narrative pieces focus on a meaningful encounter between a human and a cephalopod. All over the world, in liminal spaces between earth, air, and sea—on the shore, by a tidepool, on a dock, on a boat, while swimming, while diving, in an aquarium, in a lab—so many human beings are having a moment with a cephalopod, which gives me some hope for humanity. Of all the things human beings could be doing, including the destruction and violence we know we are capable of, these poems of engaged interspecies encounter are a testament to what is best in us, whatever the tone or ending of the particular poem.

Some poems feature speakers longing to be a cephalopod, or take on a first-person perspective: human mirror neurons firing empathetically like a squid's reflective iridophores. Sometimes a cephalopod makes only a brief appearance in a poem, expanding our perspective. Sometimes the cephalopod is only a metaphor: a way of describing human-perceived things to other humans, a felt affinity through similarity. (I wonder if a cephalopod would find our metaphors strange? Or perhaps our tentacular grappling with love or loss, ink and escape, would translate better across species, thanks to the borrowed cephalopodic imagery?)

A note on scientific accuracy: The facts and wonderings of these poems were as true as each writer knew at the time of writing, but humans are always discovering new information about cephalopods, as well as about themselves. Both science

and poetry are driven by questions, sounding out from what
is known to what might be: we can learn something even from
a not-quite-right hypothesis. By the time you read this, likely
new cephalopod information will have emerged. Are they really
color-blind, or are they actually perceiving colors with their
whole bodies? Though often solitary, what about the discovery of
octopus cities and communal nurseries? What new cephalopod
species are yet to be found in the oceanic depths? We already
look forward to future cephalopod discoveries and poems.

Some of the poems may seem antiquated in the way they
describe a cephalopod more coldly or as an objectified "it"—
rather than engaging in a "grammar of animacy": indigenous
scientist and writer Robin Wall Kimmerer's term for using the
same personal pronouns and language we would use to describe
human-people to describe our fellow non-human beings as well,
acknowledging our relationship as interrelated "kin." This kind
of poem feels important to preserve in the fossil record too.
If a cuttlefish anthropologist reads this book someday, I hope
they will be willing to look past our more occluded, human-
centric biases to appreciate our better qualities. After all our
careful scientific and lyrical study of cephalopods, we were the
specimen all along.

I believe poetry is radical possibility in language, whether
appearing as line breaks or sentences, comics or shapes
inhabiting the page. Perhaps this is another way we are like
cephalopods: in poetry, we have the potential to unfurl in every
possible direction, to perceive multidimensionally, and to squish
free (if our beak will fit) beyond the limits of our individual
human form.

Sierra Nelson, Editor
Seattle, 2024

Three Hearts

Claire Hsu Accomando

Nautilus Envy

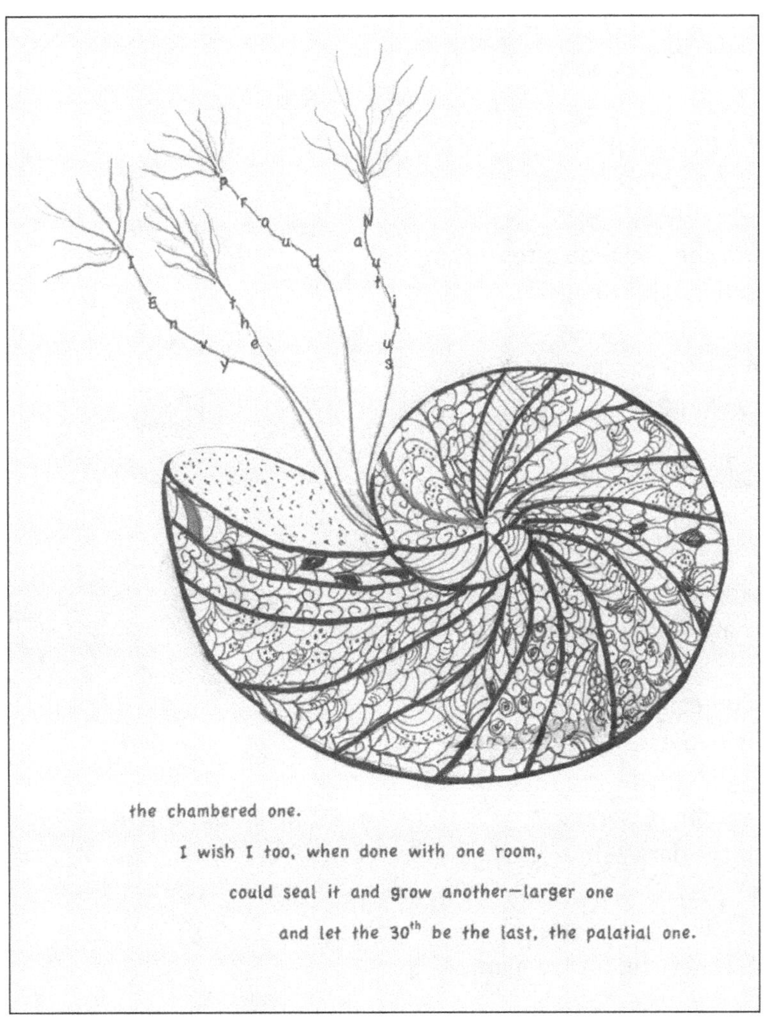

Sally Albiso

Flotsam

This morning an octopus
coils on the beach,

a glutinous pile
of dissolving limbs.

Did she succumb after mating
and hatching eggs?

A fate once commonplace
to women—

death by childbirth.
How tenuous those months

of waiting, the labor
that could go wrong:

a breeched delivery,
bleeding, fever

and life loosening
in the dark center

of a womb, the cries
of other children, a man.

No one weeps for the octopus,
the tracks of an eagle

splayed nearby,
malingering gulls.

She'll feed them now
suctioned only to wind,

no matter the number of arms
or how hard she once clung.

Sally Albiso

Keeping Vigil

Naked but for a gown,
you look like someone else's husband,
vulnerable, near sighted, wedding ring
removed. They wheel you down halls
with endless horizons
as if you're going to sea once more:
your letters still echoing in a trunk
though my responses gone.

What did I write you?
How I entered the empty house
still smelling of sleep and coffee,
rinsed out your cup and cried?
How I pulsed like a clock
ticking off hours as I do now
left behind in this room named for waiting
while you sail beneath a surgeon's scalpel.

The day before we watched
a giant octopus sleep,
tentacles tucked beneath its mantle,
eyelids closed. The octopus
remained still as simulated rock
but we lingered there
as if it were a multi-limbed god,
might bestow some grace:

relieve the pain you'll quantify
on a scale of one to ten
while I'm handed a number
to track your procedure like a flight
and ask, when you wake, if you remember

the octopus. How it opened one eye
and regarded the glimmer of our rings
attracted to shiny bits like crows.

Amy Ash

Chapodiphobia: Fear of Octopi

Octopuses is the correct plural term, I learn. I don't even know
how to name this fear that works its way over ocean floor

through pelagic waters, coral reef. Its movements quick
and unpredictable, arms curling like ribbons, body almost pink,

translucent, like a child's balloon. I see right through it,
understand its intentions, what it wants, what it will drag

and pierce and break. How can it have three hearts and still
not love me? So many arms, refusing embrace. What I fear

most is its ability to fill any space. Without bones,
it works its way into anything, seeping in and expanding,
like cancer, like grief.

M. C. Aster

Octopoidal Elegy

On a whim someone dropped
Letters and numbers into

An octopus's tank—and used his
Picks to bet on football matches.

Soon photogs couldn't get enough
Of the cephalopod's closeups.

But alas, the fisherman who kept
Him thought the joke was done

And he sold the predicting octopod
To a master sushi chef who turned

The media darling into a plate of
Artfully arranged *omakase* for

A thrilled diner who joyfully
Cried into his sake, unaware

That a small octopian star
Was dimming with each
Delicious swallow.

Hadara Bar-Nadav

Three-Hearted Love

My friend A. tells me an octopus has three hearts, and I am in
love, imagining hearts on top of hearts, this beautiful monster
three-hearted and then million-hearted. Tentacles lined with
thousands of heart-shaped suction cups. Eight legs rippling like
typewriter ribbons or like calligraphy ribboning across the ocean.
Blue blood, blue-hearted. Blue on top of blue: titian, cerulean,
pupil. Then I pause. Stop the poem.

Does this mean the octopus has three hearts full of love and also
three hearts full of emptiness? Does it swim through oceans
thinking of its hearts as full empty full empty? *Octopuses are highly
intelligent,* says my 6-year-old son. Does the octopus think in
terms of love and emptiness, does it feel love and emptiness as it
draws in water through its siphon (full) and blows it out to propel
itself forward (empty)?

Is a heart ever really full of love? The idea of love. The idea of a
heart. All symbol, clot. But I can feel the weight of it, expanding
inside my chest wall, rootbound, heavy, rolling forward like a baby.

Can one heart die while the other hearts live? Do they make a
heart family that dines on a daily bloodfeast?

When my son cries, I tell him to think of his Play-Doh as half
empty or half full. I tell him about *reframing*—a strategy from
my therapist who says, *We can't change the hard things, but we can
change how we think about them.* The Play-Doh is half full, and my
son can still play with it. My son still exists, even though his baby
sister died inside of me.

The poem doesn't continue. Blunted, misshapen, something blue
tumbles out.

The octopus has three chances for its hearts to implode or survive. To beat themselves over and over and over. Until they stop.

Cathy Barber

Otherworldly

In the animal kingdom of tigers, eagles, foxes,
within that menagerie, is the singular octopus—
a creature some say was planted, dropped
on Earth by aliens. Does it study our world,
examine it in a mini-laboratory deep
in the home it has embellished? The octopus's
intelligence, striking; its lifespan, a brief
five years. Our loss, too. Perhaps they dream
of return to their home on a clear summer night,
their water-filled spaceship shooting past our moon.

Nicky Beer

Ad Hominem

The Poet:

> Fugitive lung, prodigal intestine—where's the pink crimp in
> my side where they took you out?

The Octopus:

> It must be a dull world, indeed, where everything appears
> to be a version or extrapolation of you.
>
> The birds are you.
> The springtime is you.
> Snails, hurricanes, saddles, elevators—
> everything becomes
> you.
>
> I, with a shift
> of my skin, divest my self
> to become the rock
> that shadows it.
>
> Think of when
> your reading eyes momentarily drift,
> and in that instant
>
> you see the maddening swarm of alien ciphers submerged
>   within the text
> gone before you can focus. That's me.
>
> Or your dozing revelation
> on the subway that you are slowly being
> digested. Me again.

I am the fever dream
in which you see your loved ones
as executioners. I am also their axe.

Friend, while you're exhausting
the end of a day
with your sad approximations,

I'm a mile deep
in the earth, vamping
my most flawless impression of the abyss

to the wild applause of eels.

Nicky Beer

Frost on the Octopus

*The blue-ringed octopus is one of the most poisonous animals
in the world.*

She is as at the fair both circus tent
and sideshow freak within, each blue-ringed spot
an ornament and affliction intent
on advertising, in the polyglot
speech of nature, her peculiar venom
which seizes the victim first in a rush
of wonderment, freezing his limbs in some sudden winter,
    all the while a weird thrush mottles
his tongue with rime, so that his first words of love should be
    perfectly preserved
for this tattooed girl, this contortionist
adrift in the lonely excess of her
power, so rife with death throughout she will
at times, upon her own breath, taste its chill.

Ahimsa Timoteo Bodhrán

Entreaty: invite from the ocean floor

Round, it swells, bells,
cling, clangs the vibration; clink, clank. We pray here.
Resonant vessels vacillate. If each dancer vibrates
the ocean of the other's body, locate, for me,
the shore. Is there a rudder? Sequence
my star chart. Navigate our nearness.
Astrolabe the archipelago.
Kelp, bubbling, bends; wavering, weaves.
Fish school. Cephalopods, inky,
congregate; jellyfish pulse, prod
the prurient; anemone undulate, briny billow;
coral, advance and retreat. Faults realign, magma
multiplies, hydrothermals hiccup. Smokers vent.

Where are the brackish waters, where fresh
feeds salt? Tell me about your estuaries. Where is the endpoint,
upriver, where you define the end of your territory? Where the inside
of
your body pours out. Each orifice, Möbius, sea-cucumbering.
We reveal our innards to those we most love. Violence,
a violation because it pierces the body without consent, brings
the outside in, unbidden. *I did not say you could enter this body.*
Surgeons slice the sway. They correct the oceans. Retill
the currents. Choreographers, we need water wizards working
the wells. Folk who can re-freeze, glacial, the ice, turn us blue
again.

What water wisdom do you know? How does it weave with mine?
Show me, here, now.

Karina Borowicz

Fist

The octopus frightened me the first time
I saw it—I didn't believe
something so strange lived even in a place
I couldn't see.

It flew forcefully through the water
a human hand gesturing
with a dancer's confidence and sometimes
the anger of a fist.

I stood before the tank in the darkened room
beads of spotlight scattering
upon the water's surface
the heavier oil of light
plunging down into that square of cold sea.

Janet Bowdan

Octavia and the Joke

A writer, a researcher, and a reporter
walk into a lab to pet the octopus,
Octavia, who propels herself over to meet them,
holds out her arms for them
to stroke—they say she's soft,
like custard, but a coral red.
If she were in the ocean, she'd be walking
across the sand using her arms as legs,
she'd prey on small sharks
but she's made friends here.

While I'm trying to find a way into this poem,
Octavia's trying to find a way out. She's
clever that way. I can't tell whether
she's trying to pull one over
on her visitors or whether it's a joke
she's sharing with us—pulling our legs, so to speak.
Nothing up her sleeves, all eight
of her lovely tentacles.

If I had more arms, I'd make dinner faster;
I'd throw baseballs for the boys to catch;
I'd juggle. How would my two-handed brain keep up
with my multiplied hands? Octavia's
brain wraps around her throat,
impels her to reach out
unseen for the bucket of fish, so when they look
around to reward her with a treat, it's gone,
she's snaffled it with two arms while they
were stroking the three they saw.

If she gets bored, if we don't watch out,
she might just slip out of her exhibit, turn up in another tank
to eat the inhabitants, or open valves, or
disassemble the expensive equipment just
to amuse herself.

The sound of water hums in the tank,
imagined octopus the color of dark ocean
lulled and carried along by currents.
And now Octavia reveals the bucket
full of fish she's tucked away under
some of her arms, waiting to show off her prize.

Elizabeth Bradfield

Sweater for a Giant Squid

    after a sculpture by Mary Carlson

And now I see how bare the body is, how fleshy,
all underbelly and membrane, all slick
and interior. Pull its tentacles
into the long, long sleeves. Hood
its large eyes. Clothe it. Make it

decent. Hide us from the shocking bareness
of its eight bare arms.

There are a few other things that could stand
to be clothed—

raccoons splayed
along the roadside, chicken breasts
in cellophane, my fear that love will leave
me, new buds swelling from the maple,

that dream I had last night, ripped
through the warm cardigan of dark.

Ronda Piszk Broatch

It was the year of considering time travel,

and how to save the North Atlantic Right Whale.
Spring is ending, and SpaceX will tuck baby bobtail squid

and tardigrades inside its Dragon cargo capsule.
What I didn't realize is there might be thousands of tardigrades

already on the moon. Because octopuses are so intelligent,
a brain in each arm, eating them feels cannibalistic.
Some say the octopus is what an alien might look like.

When you say that aliens might not be interested in us,
I say I understand we have a lot to learn, a lot to undo.

There is dust behind the stars, some stiff-hipped moths
circling the drain of my poorly draining shower.
Without electromagnetic fields, gamma rays, radio waves,

we are blind. Imagine alien physicists doing calculations
in a dark matter lab. It was the year of reading late,

of conducting thought experiments, and getting lost
in seawater with cephalopods. The year of silver linings,
of watching the red disappear from my hair until it wisps

ghost-like around my eyes. If not for dark matter, what of
the aliens we so wish to contact? It was a virus year,

a year of feeling alien in our skins. If not for baby squids
and the myriad tardigrades drifting in the blackness above
our heads, if not for you, then why be dazzled?

Rebecca Brock

Octopus

  after Sarah Wilson & Kay Redfield Jamison

To conquer a beast,
so the old Chinese proverb goes,
you must first make it beautiful—
offering latitude or space,
let's call it language, for naming
what ails and aches, what rattles
clear through the great gaping maw
shifting shape
like something not human—
bleeds blue, beats three hearts
and thinks with feeling clear through the whole,
each arm—longing and loosening
the way it blends, changes skin
not just color but tone, texture, shape—
what is there to say, at the end then
when asked: who are you, what are you,
what did you desire? How to say
without speaking: I didn't know.
And what would it be to say: I danced
and spun and dove
in the ether
and didn't ever know
the limits
of my own skin.

Meg Caldwell

Our Lady of Mollusks

> *"Molly, our 27-foot-long preserved giant squid, is finally home.*
> *Molly was accidentally caught by a deep-sea commercial fishing*
> *trawler off the southeastern coast of New Zealand in 1999, she was*
> *then donated to Mote."*
> — *Mote Marine Laboratory and Aquarium*

White skin dressed in formaldehyde,
when I make the cross in the doorway to the exhibit
have I created you as saint? As relic? As religion?
You have always been myth, you never minded
sailors didn't believe in you until they found you
washed up on their beaches, Goddess put on display
for my fat child fingers to gawk, to try
and understand your body under glass.

My own hajj to the aquarium, from circling
your glass tank, rushing towards living snook black
lines down white bodies, ignoring your tragedy for sand
shark and nurse shark, for manta ray and mangrove fish.
It took me so long to convert, to finally recognize you
as deity I thought of crucifixion as form of forever.

Your resting places have moved, the scientists
studied your casket within their lab and displayed your
body in exhibit after exhibit until finally
moving you into the room holding your shrine.

The body you knew from the before
painted in a mural above you, red
like poppies fluttering on the wall, you were the color
of blood meeting oxygen, how could you have hidden
for so long in such an extravagant scarlet?

Informative plaques nailed to the walls of the room
explain to viewers what you were, are, directing us
to the windows of your casket
where you've transformed to
ghost white and continue to shrink in size.

Would you have preferred to decompose like your kin?
Drift down through the miles of ocean, finally hitting the bottom
where isopods would harvest you from the inside out?
From myth, to apex predator, to food for bacteria, krill,
     sea cucumbers,
living on in something so small.

When I look at you now
I wonder when you became sacrament.
I leave my shoes at the doorway of your temple,
I cross my torso when I walk in.
I kneel to get a better glimpse of your body.
Sometimes I mistake my position for prayer.

Beach Walk

<pre>
                    we
               walk a wild
             beach quiet wide
           expanse of gray wavy
          sand rolling saltwater far
         in the distance extreme low
         tide splashing over stacked
           rocks   sea stars orange
            pink anemones tightly
           shut swaying kelp forest
           nursery   baby crabs hidden
        cephalopods shifting to wavery
         green fronds rippling   tree shapes
       rolling peach   charcoal   taupe specks
       my sis bends   retrieves   from beach
       a perfect ecru   spiraling   moon snail
        turns it back   and forth   in briny air
         inside I see   arms curl   dark wriggle
          I grab her   thin wrist   my sis gasps
           dropping   the home   a spiral shell
            onto the   striated   buff shore
            small   grayish   Octopoda
            scoots   under   a rock half
            buried   by the   shifting
            sand   grains   the sea's
          gift   we hug   giddy
         &   happy   alike
</pre>

Kersten Christianson

Oceanic

Whitecaps
rule this day
of minus.
Wind's folly

blasts the crest
before the plunge.
The day's sun
flutters, an errant

octopus tripping
below the surface
like my anxious
heart.

Joanne M. Clarkson

Broken Heart Syndrome

At last I believe my own pain. The clench
from chest to jaw and shoulder.
And after rooms of glaring
light and tube after tube
of purloined blood, someone writes
Takotsubo cardiomyopathy
on the diagnosis line. Aka *broken
heart syndrome*

transmitted within the hormone mix
of women. Left ventricle, the main pumping
chamber, ballooned beyond rhythm
by the aftermath of ruin: relationship,
savings, earthquake, flood, fire, faith.

Takotsubo is not, as I presumed, the surname
of a scientist or physician. It is a Japanese
octopus trap. Simple fishing pot
into which a being of nine minds
wanders. A protracted death, squeezing,
shooting, pounding, cannibal agony

for the sake of an unnecessary
banquet. At the thought of the beautiful
creature consumed, my heart contracts
and the old aching creeps down

my left arm to fingers never taught how
to spring the trap. I will not write here
what captured me, unawares. Which personal
demon incited the chemicals signaling
my involuntary muscle. There is no

treatment but time. Heaps of brightly painted
cannisters tossed onto docks at nightfall.
And in the phosphorescent sea,
the fate of my own healing.

Will Cordeiro

Homage to Inky, Escapee from the National Aquarium of New Zealand

Mottled matter
       of a too-smooth
              butterface, a mood-

hued hacker who
       wears a brain
              on each sleeve

is giving you the slip,
       tentacles torquing,
              crack as a whip-

smart ship-in-a-bottle;
       he kisses his tank
              -mate goodbye as

he hip-swivels &
       Houdinis out in a
              prisonbreak: shape

-shifting jelly, jerry-rigged
       soft body figuring elisions
              & pivots. As if solving cross-

words or Sudoku,
       he unscrews a cap
              left slightly ajar—

buckles & warps,
        balloons with his go-
                to move of a kip up,

crabwalks then top
        -rocks himself over-
                board: bard of all gut

squeezing & crazy 8
        footwork, scatter-
                brained mentalist

bending a spoon:
        this latter-day skin
                -walker or aswang

who assumes, willy-nilly,
        the form of an heirloom
                tomato or spermatozoon.

Now scooting off
        & having nothing
                to frame him, half

poet, half parrotfish
        manqué, spilling head-
                goo, he oozes out

the radius of a tube
        from the arid hallucination
                of his lockbox's pelagic

zone; edges his taut
        flanks flat before
                he enters the un-

sanctioned vacuum of
        air; strategizing through
                its vanishing oculus,

Inky slinks, straddling
        thick plexiglass. Next
                suctions, next bellycrawls

across tiled floor;
        glides down the trickle
                of a drainpipe, rallying

to be swiped back
        to ride deep fathoms
                & lathering sea tides.

Brittany Corrigan

Fossil Record: Ammonite

Words nestled in the chambers of my brain, not
numbers, which refused to suture themselves to me,

my neurons tentacling after them, floating through
the murky deep. Though I did like geometry—a class

in which our teacher stood on his head to keep us rapt
as points turned to lines, curves ellipsed across the page.

But calculus nearly did me in, and formulas in college
science labs spiraled me back to the buoyancy of language,

grammar re-shelling me in the coils of its arms. Until
the Fibonacci sequence awoke what I had let go dark:

the wonder of nature's mathematics, perfection of petals,
webs, and seeds. The golden ratio radiates through

siphuncle and septa as ammonoid bodies surface across
glaciers and plains. Once abundant in all of Earth's oceans,

defying three extinctions before their meteoric end, they've never
needed us to name them, date them, index their molluskan forms.

But I needed to explode my mind around their mineral sums:
my world expanding further and further, beyond measure.

Kevin Craft

Linear B

I've etched each phoneme
of your name into this
my most beautiful vase.
Some seal their *kraters* with poly-
chrome fire, others with a kiss.

And so it goes with octopuses
whose beaks can crack a mollusk;
who, startled, release
quick clouds of ink, escaping
into self-made dusk.

Beyond the sinkhole
of love and fame, I've no more
reliable appliance.
I dally in the harbor, daubing
starfish on faience.

Count your figs and figurines.
Secure the harried latch
to the storeroom whose great *pithoi*
mock our losses, love. If only
we could start from scratch.

John Davis

Cartilaginous Craniums

O so social
shoaling with fish
flying through air
jet propelled
water expelled from funnels
spreading tentacles like wings
in a flat fan shape

Spy on squid in the dark
and you will find their flight pattern
I might invite and dine with them
on my dive though they shine light
downward to disguise their shadows
expel ink to detract predators

Sheathed hooks   keels
funnel mantle fusion
can't get enough of fin holes
and suckers
If I had balance sensory receptors
I could detect gravity
outswim a shark

could flick my tentacle
like the waved hand
of a debutante
flaunt my body posture
be a countershade or firefly
bloom like an iris

Claire Dawson

Eight Ways of Looking

Octopuses have a brain in each arm, I hear, not
a real one but something basic and elegant, just the essentials.
Enough to hunt a little, to create a sweep of that arm's radar
so as to keep abreast of the nearest events in what must
be a world divided into quadrants. Octants. A faceted world
of eightfoldness that swirls around like a vast and liquid
kaleidoscope. What would it be like, do you think, for your
hands to give you their report of the day, your feet to gently
suggest that maybe it was time you thought about standing a
little less on the hard floors, or perhaps investing in a pumice stone?
Would your fingers have things to say about the way you never
seem to come to the end of the dishes, or how they love the feel
of loam and smooth stones? Maybe they'd go out hunting for you,
too, and come back to show you all the things they had found.
To remind you that, every day, there are eight new worlds
just waiting for you to come looking.

Lynn Domina

Human Questions for an Observant Octopus

Does your beauty require symmetry? Or do you evaluate other
    beings by their buoyancy?

Do you dream something stalks you, always just out of sight?

When you eat a cuttlefish that has just eaten a small octopus,
    does rage or revenge influence your hunger? Have you ever
    felt guilty for eating another sentient being?

Have you ever dreamed of falling? Have you ever fallen? When
    you dream of falling, what do you try to catch hold of?

Do you fall asleep to the music of whales singing?

Does your language include words for predator or prey?

When you grow bored with your appearance, what do you change?

Does your head ache? Do you feel a dull throb or sharp spike at
    the base of your skull?

When you relax, do you allow your arms to drift with the current?
    Does this remind you of infinity?

Does infinity attract you? Is your ocean infinite? Which infinity
    would you choose, space or time?

Timothy Donnelly

Panspermia

```
a    i    l    a    a    t    t    a    r    c    y    y    c    y
p    t    e    l    n    h    o    n    e    o    o    o    a    o
r    d    s    o    i    e    a    d    l    n    u    u    g    u
a    o    s    n    n    e    n    i    e    t    w    a    h    f
 y   e    l    e    d    a    e    t    a    r    h    r    h    i
e    s    i    i    o    e    r    l    g    s    o    a    e   t   n
r    n    g    t    n    n    o    s    o    e    l    t    a   w   d
m    t    a    l    a    t    f    e    e    i    w    y    e   d   i   y
i    a    t    a    m    a    a    w    s    t    h    o    v   r   t   o
g    l    u    n    o    t    n    h    l    y    i    u    e   o   h   u
h    w    r    d    u    i    a    e    i    o    c    r    r   p   o   r
t    a    e    s    n    o    n    r    k    u    h    s    m   l   u   s
e    y    t    w    t    n    i    e    e    c    w    e    i   e   t   e
n    s    h    h    a    i    m    a    t    a    a    l    g   t   w   l
d    g    a    e    i    n    a    c    h    n    s    f    h   l   a   f
u    o    n    r    n    t    l    o    i    t    l    i    t   i   r   h
p    w    b    e    o    h    n    i    s    r    i    n    b   t   n   e
a    h    r    i    r    e    o    l    f    e    k    t    e   b   i   l
n    e    o    t    d    s    t    e    o    e    e    o    a   r   n   d
y    r    a    l    o    o    o    d    r    l    l    t    r   i   g   i
w    e    d    a    w    i    f    a    n    i    y    h    m   e   y   n
h    y    c    n    n    l    t    p    o    t    t    e    e   f   o   t
e    o    a    d    b    a    h    p    r    b    h    h    a   l   u   h
 r   u    s    s    y    n    e    e    e    a    e    a    n   y   a   i
  e  m    t    a    t    e    e    n    a    c    a    n    i   o   r   s
   e      e    n    h    m    a    d    s    k    i    d    n   n   e   p
   a      a    d    e    p    r    a    o    y    m    s    g   t   c   l
   n      c    i    s    t    t    g    n    o    a    o    n   h   a   u
   f      h    t    e    i    h    e    b    u    l    f    o   e   r   r
   o      m    c    a    n    a    a    u    s    l    w    t   b   r   a
   r      o    a         e    n    l    t    u    a    h    h   a   i   l
   i      r    t         s    e    o    n    r    l    a    i   c   e   i
   t      p    c         s    n    n    o    r    o    t    n   k   d   t
   t      h    h         i    t    g    l    e    n    e    g   f   i   y
  o o     e    e         n    r    t    e    u    n    g    v   s   u   n o
  g r     m    s         t    y    e    s    n    d    t    e   t   r   a f
  o g     e    o         h    n    s    a    e    o    r    a   o   l   l
   o      a    r         e    t    v    r    t    m    t    f   l   i
   t      s    i         s    a    o    h    i    i    n    d   f
   h      e    t         h    c    i    r    g    s    i    i   e
   e      e    d         a    l    d    o    h    t    g    r
   r      d    o         p    e    a    w    t    i    h    e
   e           e         e    a    b    c    c    t    c
   o           s         o    h    l    o    a    a    o    t
   n           n         f    o    y    n    t    l    r    i
    l          t         r    c    c    l    o
    y                    n    e    h    y    n
                         y         s
                         o
                         u
```

Merridawn Duckler

Life of Octopus

Crawling or by propulsion, solitary or sharing the crevice,
with what was food, but survived the paralyzing kiss
and stays, companionable, in the seagrass floor.

The head and nine brains engorge one end,
the arms feel light and touch without stereognosis.
The little cups make their guesses.
The vast ocean is small to them, reflected in dark waters,
nominating arms model a blue globe.

The male moves into her mantels
waxing sand or coral-colored,
neither tough nor tender
all secrets begin in pleasure,

in eggs hung in strands in mottled caves
like frozen bubbles, she watches them with the true love
of guardianship of the immortal gene.
Undulates
her beautiful creation
of no particular beauty,
sees and cleans
and then dies of starvation.

He died long ago.
In solo, among the salt waves, the orphan planktonic
emerge and dangle in water in the pattern of *passing cloud*,
a camouflage both prescriptive and descriptive.

In the shallows against predators,
an arm investigating mortality can break off,
or pour into the tiniest circle

of existence: death, solitude, slow ecstasy
to be a thing beyond
the strict borders of things.

Liza Katz Duncan

Kraken

my name means
twisted, unsound

i am background
i am scrim

see how quickly
i disappear into
something else:

the alone in abalone
the i in island

i cannot be reached

sex is a hell
of harsh water

a degenerate current
refracted
through me

when he finishes
i am so so hungry

let no man make
myth of me

let no one
monster me
out of existence

say my name and
i crescendo

say my name and
i slicken

i cyclone
i whirlpool

i starburst
into open air

Camille T. Dungy

Characteristics of Life

> *A fifth of animals without backbones could be at risk*
> *of extinction, say scientists.*
>> —*BBC Nature News*

Ask me if I speak for the snail and I will tell you
I speak for the snail.
                          I speak of underneathedness
and the welcome of mosses,
                                      of life that springs up,
little lives that pull back and wait for a moment.

I speak for the damselfly, water skeet, mollusk,
the caterpillar, the beetle, the spider, the ant.
                                      I speak
from the time before spinelessness was frowned upon.

Ask me if I speak for the moon jelly. I will tell you
                  one thing today and another tomorrow
      and I will be as consistent as anything alive
on this earth.

                  I move as the currents move, with the breezes.
What part of your nature drives you? You, in your cubicle
ought to understand me. I filter and filter and filter all day.

Ask me if I speak for the nautilus and I will be silent
as the nautilus shell on a shelf. I can be beautiful
and useless if that's all you know to ask of me.

Ask me what I know of longing and I will speak of distances
      between meadows of night-blooming flowers.

                                    I will speak
              the impossible hope of the firefly.

                                    You with the candle
burning and only one chair at your table must understand
         such wordless desire.

              To say it is mindless is missing the point.

Leanne Dunic

Salt Rich

Nearby, a combat ship sank. Divers retrieved bags of flour smelling of fungus, tasting of sea. During the war, villagers evaporated brine in limestone hollows. Night fishermen held lanterns overboard to attract octopuses. Used their tridents. Ocean alive: sea cucumbers, urchins, squid, sea horses. Easy to get meat from limpets, sea snails. The slick inside of a fish—gut odor indelible on fingers. Salt lines the skin.

Natalie Dupille

Northwest Homegrown

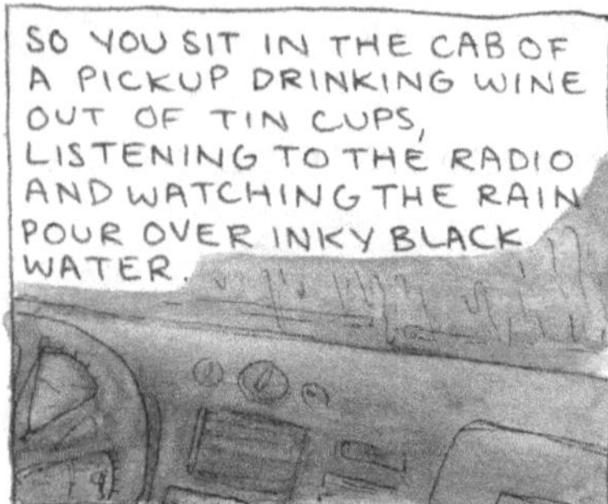

SQUID ARE BEST CAUGHT IN RAINY, CLOUDY WEATHER BUT ON NIGHTS LIKE THIS ONE IT'S TOO WET FOR EVEN THE SQUIDDERS TO BE OUT.
SO YOU SIT IN THE CAB OF A PICKUP DRINKING WINE OUT OF TIN CUPS, LISTENING TO THE RADIO AND WATCHING THE RAIN POUR OVER INKY BLACK WATER.

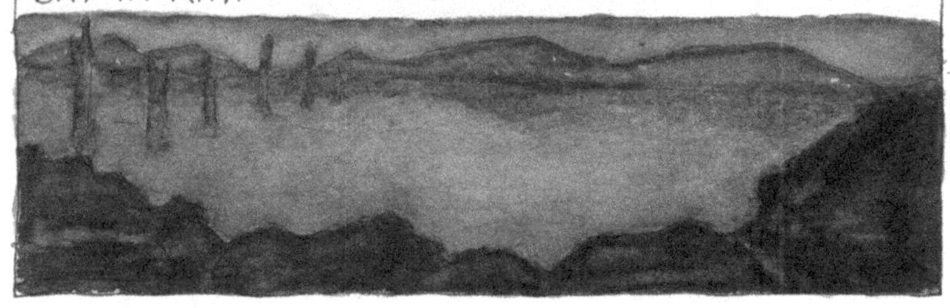

IMAGINING THE INKERS THEMSELVES MOVING NORTH AS THE SEASON ENDS, READY TO REAPPEAR IN NEAH BAY IN MAY.

46

Amy Eisner

Hunger

We were all grazing alone, then we were grazing on one
    another.   The exchange of chemicals became a danger.

Shadows urged us to pick up our feet.   We raised up parasols
        and they became beaks.   We swallowed our beaks

    and became balloons, bladders, pumps.   We gushed
        to get away from each other.   We had to know

            what was ours when we brought it
    to our mouths.   Who can say when hunger

            became hunger for what would elude our grasp?
We developed eyes and see nothing better

        than other eyes.   Then there are spots
                that seem to see back.   Imagination

        requires another.   To remain unseen
            we screen the movie of the world without us

    against our hypermorphic skins.
                We tell our dreams only to ourselves.

In every electric nest pulsing within
            fledgling thoughts nestle.   One we can't resist:

            inside the sideways-scuttling rocks can be found
    a sweetness that comes of taking shape.

Katy E. Ellis

Octopus Boy

Sometimes you are an octopus boy
        reaching all directions
                between shore stones
        sensing places that conceal
a mother, a father, a brother—
        your childhood family
                a bouquet of sargassum
        swaying for a single tide's season.

Your tentacles wand a memory flush—

        late-night arguments
                and the barnacled basketball court
        among tall pines in a newly built
                apartment complex
        and your first car a bribe
                to not drop out of school

—all but the fisheye gone to skeleton.

Sometimes you wrap every arm
        around us—your wife, your daughter
                and you give us each
        one of your three hearts
which we use to buoy your blood
        or to camouflage your heaviest wounds.

Always you hold the heart that stops beating
        when you swim, the one
                you were punished for trying to outrun
        when you were eight years old

and an ear infection funneled
        your attention—
                shush-shush
                shush-shush
—to the sound of something alive in you,
        the heart that keeps you crawling
                past the breakwater
                                into open sea.

Heather Eudy

Fuchsia Hunger

My mom calls them ballerinas—fuchsia blooms—
for their pointed toes, slender legs, explosive tutus.
Fuchsia plant pairs adorn my patio now—
red-purple dancers, white-purple dancers.
And when I need a rush, I pick one,
place ballerina extravagance on my tongue.
Sometimes I swallow her whole
like a squid—
the ones that disappear by glowing
and together we descend into nothingness.

Lynn Finger

The squid, a shadowed shawl

bloats in seaweed-drenched ropes
alongside our blue fishing trawler.

Stolen from wave shards, its limbs
criss-crossed with sinew, body taut
with a single bone, gills flare.

It thrashes, slashes at the net with sharp
arms. I lean over the side, meet its
moonless eye, and see myself in it,

coatless in the rain rash. I brought
myself aboard with no ticket,
a year ago, work for exchange,

it too is bound. Neither of us
are where we want to be.

I feel swollen apologies for it,
drained of power just because it swims
here. I hear the crew call to each other,

as they near: stuck, dredge,
drinks, cash.

I take my serrated knife in one hand,
and hold to the rail with the other.
I cut one rope with it, then two,

then a third, enough for its shoulder
to break into air, then it falls
in a mantle of eight arms, a crowd

of rain, straight down past rail and boat
and triangles of water, it dives
into black foam and blue waves, home.

The sea angles me too, I lean
towards a land with a pull I cannot
follow. Yet.
I put my knife away.

Mark A. Fisher

Haiku

nautilus shells
in logarithmic spirals
galactic echo

Amber Flame

an octopus escapes the fishing net:
advice for my daughter as cephalopod

in this life, where you must be both
predator and delicacy, rend
for yourself the tenderest bits.

enter a world, daughter
where you may drink brine and not be
pickled;

lose remorse in the hunt for that which feeds
you. be sure
there are eight passions
for each arm's embrace,
in case your dreams are injured
or cut short.

by all means, keep yourself
whole, even as you adapt with grace,

honey love. my
sinuous structure
pure musculature   and give;

infinite flex and reshaping, do not
be confined to any that would contain you.

be gentle relentless
manipulation; hang on, love,
or disappear   in the confusion of your melanin

clouding the display; how they love
to watch you squirm   and ooze;
be not object
entertainment,   remember how
to pry open exits   remember
camouflage.

learn both lurk   and listen;
eyes open to color of danger
of safety

do not forget that tucked up
in the unfurling of your
pretty petticoat of a   body:

you are thought and plot. beak
and brain. predator and delicacy.   Feed.

²⁰Ca

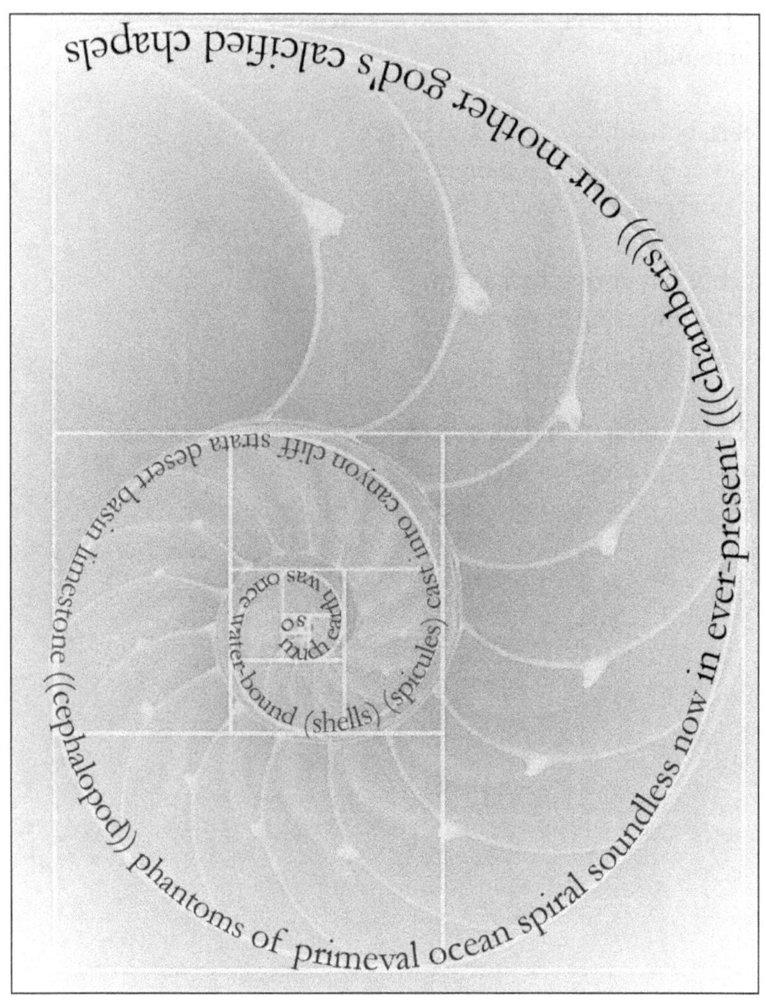
our mother god's calcified chapels
(((chambers)
now in ever-present
spiral soundless
phantoms of primeval ocean
((cephalopod))
limestone
desert basin
cast into canyon cliff strata
(spicules)
water-bound (shells)
so much earth was once

Gabriela Denise Frank

Octo-Blot

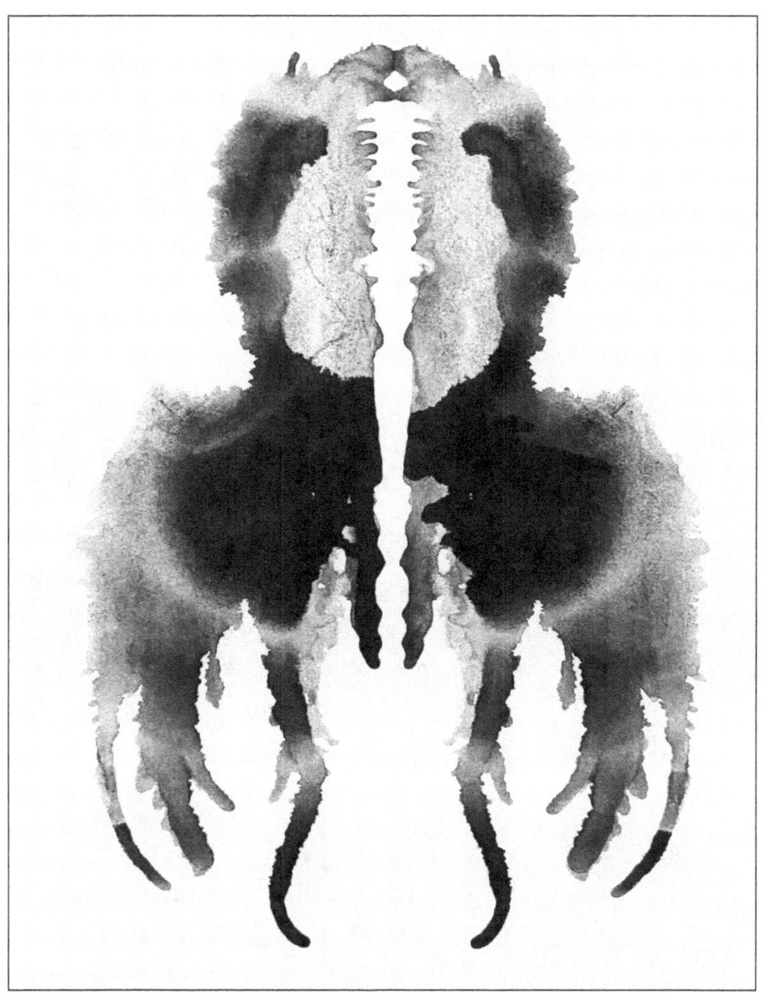

Emily Franklin

What We See

1.
How about that time we stood off-season in wet sand as waves
tossed a garbage-bagged body? Cell phones didn't exist so we
discussed just how long we should stare at a murder disposed
of, tarped, and chucked before calling for help. And it's good
we talked, because while we talked the body became a harp
seal, jack-in-boxing up, carnival-eyed, all of us surprised by
being seen.

2.
Convinced we'd spotted the cephalopod from the air, we
shared a moment of secrecy on a jam-packed airplane, all of
us crated together like animals en route to a factory farm, this
creature below our own saving grace except that squid became
eco-cabanas, each pod connected, rafted, floating elegant and
marooned. We brushed off our foolishness, but as I waited for
the boxy bathroom, I saw how easily we'd been mistaken, just
how plausible our folly—mantle, tentacles, head, and arms. How
close we were to Father Island, Chichi-jima, where the only one
was caught on film, preserved, revered.

3.
What about when you swore the baby had grown a beard
overnight, transformed into a onesie-clad woodsman? And
the next night, same thing—shaggy, shedding blanket knit by
a high school friend I'd ditched before this Paul Bunyan baby
insisted on growing downy facial hair in her basinet. We gave
away the blanket soon after. Now maybe someone else sees
what we saw. Whatever we think we see is what we see.

Kelly Froh

Ink Adventure

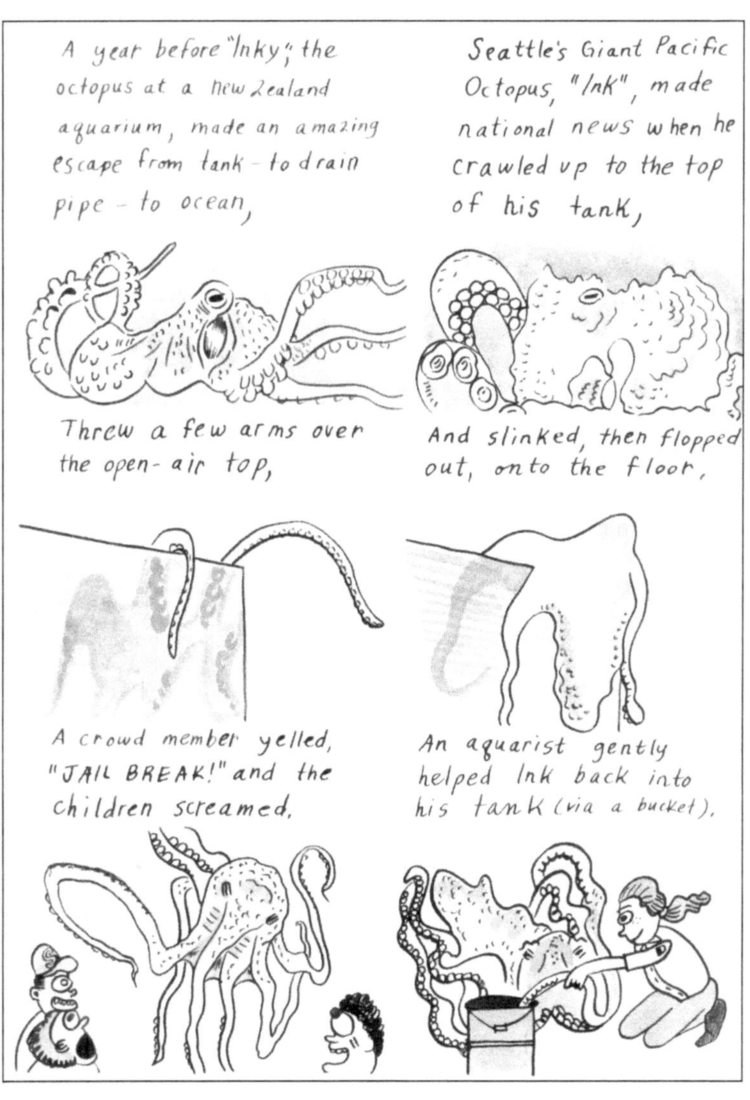

The media, when reporting with puns (as they do) "So Long, Suckers," emphasized the "escape",

But an aquarium spokesperson redirected the narrative with a more dignified and educational explanation;

Ink was eventually re-leased back into the Puget Sound,

as our aquarium does with all their octopuses that temporarily grace us with their precense.

Sarah Kilch Gaffney

Northern Life

As a small child, I sat
at my grandparents' table,
a barnacle the size of a fist
balanced on the windowsill,
pale moon snails lined
up nearby as the sun
tracked through the sky
and the fog descended,
dull shells lovely
in the dusky light,
like most northern life,
but inside a nautilus,
deep sea dreamer
of warmer latitudes,
a different kind of spiral
like windows into light,
glimmer and pearl, but
seen only when the shell
is open, split wide.

Heidi Geis

Floaters

Once upon a time, an eye doctor was impressed by the large number of eye floaters I have. Sometimes they are all I can see. Sometimes I check myself for pain in case this time my retina really has detached. I read that an increase in floaters is a sign of retinal detachment. Most of the time, I don't notice the floaters. My brain just ignores them. When I'm tired or stressed, they are all I can see. They become a type of invisibility. A way to disappear while still being there, like a squid glowing to not be seen.

Dean Gessie

octopus in the room

the diagnosis is like gravity falling
you slide your weight against the hospital wall
it feels exactly like that bout of sunstroke
how you keeled over, arms flailing
waking to snow blindness and avalanche burial

well, this is a shitty turn of events
the self-talk is a distancing device
salty language and toilet humour are
precursors to double-fisted road rage
Jesus, what are we going to do?

oh, boy, there's another hazard in the water
what you said after learning you couldn't have children
what you *will* say, sort of, in the last stage of his sickness
when he becomes both child and umbilical cord
Jesus, what am i going to do?

later, his wound opens like an evil flower
he conjugates pornographic locutions
to describe an imaginary *other* in perfect
parallel structure—grinding, contorting, licking
how he never gave you the *real skinny*

but you've taken your vaccinations
you know he resents your perfect brain
trundles out tall tales of revenge porn
for his pseudonymous writers group of one
launches knives and arrows and darts
practices the black arts of near impalement

you catch as catch can as carnival queen
and suicide care-giver
busk your grief like a puppeteered prop
regale passersby with sobbing and convulsing
a hundred year rain event become
an all-seasonal affective disorder
your mouth a hat for ducats and gratuities
your body a caterpillar of advancing muscular sorrow

and you creep into the bedroom
like a dead thing or a battered woman
make a crucible and tomb of the rutting place
and compress beneath your weight the piles
of student papers you have neatly arranged there

of course, if you were sensible to human suffering
you might see the similarity between yourself
as de facto narrator of your own Greek goat song
and that greedily smoking, blood-letting heroine of
By Grand Central Station I Lay Down and Wept

but your lover has taken an octopus brain for his consort
lobes of mimicry, reflexive intimidation and inky camouflage
and you suffer blows as slow-motion oxidyzer
	for vacuum bombs
multiple aerosol clouds of shrieking shrapnel that penetrate
the risibly soft conduits of memory and hope

to see it any other way would be *dementia*

Jessica Gigot

Epitaph for an Octopus

When Paul, the prophetic
cephalopod died, I cried.

Beauty is born from a balance
between expansive freedom
and a clear boundary.

Before each game
the Germans hung flags
on each end of your tank.
You would prophesy the winning team
by placing your long, tentacled
arm on the glass.

I forget the spaciousness of living in water,
adhesion always against the skin.
The buoyancy of constant belonging.

I still believe in you, bottom dweller,
even though you are gone.
I covet your three harmonized hearts, titan brain
and easy grace.

My body juts through air
with just these two awkward limbs.
Space along my side for more touch,
room left in my chest for more heart.

Gabby Gilliam

Subclass Coleoidea

If I had three hearts
I could tuck

your voice
your laugh
your smile

into one
and let

the others compensate
for its fractured beat

cut through this sea
with a skirt made of fin

use my cuttlebone to drain
water when I feel like I'm drowning

train my skin to look
like something else

something settled
in its surroundings

a steady stone
unmoved by the tide.

Gabby Gilliam

There Are Hawaiian Squid in Space

Three inch cephalopods
adrift in the inky blackness
above our atmosphere.

Do they feel at home
as they swim, microgravity
their artificial ocean

is the universe a vast sea
each star a beacon
of bioluminescence

can those hobnails hum
as luciferin meets oxygen
emit cosmic communications

through chemical reaction
a spaceship of tiny stars
reaching for their giant cousins

hosts of symbiotic bacteria
meet burning balls of gas?

Terry Godbey

I Fell in Love with an Octopus

I fell in love with an octopus
though we never touched. He swam
to the side of his tank, waggled
a couple of arms at me. I pressed
my index finger to the cold glass.
He pressed a suction cup
to my finger, waved his other arms
in a hula, would not turn his slitted eyes
from mine. After many minutes, my husband
urged me to move on.
There are plenty more fish
in the sea. I stepped to the right.
The octopus followed.
I think this octopus is in love with me,
I said, thinking an eight-armed paramour
might have certain advantages.
This was before
I read about a lonely octopus
who opened a valve one night
and overflowed his tank. Before
I discovered an octopus
has three hearts
and I lack one. Before
I learned that, when threatened,
I, too, release
a cloud of black ink.

Adriana Grant

octopus

a coup, a scoop, sometimes a swallow,
a pouting taco, loco, one flew over
the cuckoo's nest, on the cusp of poco,
this many-armed creature is a liquid
scoop of soup, a spout of intention, faster
than you might imagine, the octopus
is an eight-legged swimmer, a purse
with water inhaled and expulsed,
and, on land, it looks a monster, its
thin tentacles reaching out, reaching, a
lace pattern of speed out of the
water. tentacles against sand, breath-
held, and a soup, a coup, a cup
scuttling out of the air, a scout and
out, in, a scoot, the tapas of the
sand now under, under water, and all
legs, all legs back to the sea,
under and waving, under and inhaling
the water, under and safe.

Lee Guylas

Deep Sea

> *The deep sea is often described as "a world of eternal darkness."*
> *That is a lie.*
>
> —Biologist Edie Widder

Blue streaks, arcing embers, luciferous
flares in puffs like smoke to shine the way,

how the sparks that flood the abyssal deep
become self-made stars.

The iridescence in the bay comes from Noctiluca,
tiny single-celled algae that float under

the surface of the water and glow
when disturbed. But then the deep

sea biologist comes to town and shows
pictures from the ocean floor, inky map

of animal phantasms.
Some blaze from green to blue,

counter-illuminating to evade predators. Eerie
siphonophores attract whole fish

with raw red lures, another hunts
with long spirals of poisonous tentacles

reaching outward in glowing, fluid filaments.
Firefly squid flash white during trysts

at night. Hordes of ferocious monsters
bear names like *Black-devil anglerfish*

and *Vampire squid from hell*, startling
shadow dwellers, the sinister

photons of nightmares.
Except these voracious predators

are only a few centimeters long, tiny
lights in the largest habitat on the planet.

The biologist says *In the ocean bioluminescence
is the rule rather than the exception.* The best

I can do is crack a Wint-O-Green
Life Saver in the hall closet and watch

sparks fly from my open mouth, but
when that's done I'm still in the dark.

Susan E. Hamilton

Celestial Grazing

The moon crosses rippleless water,
guides herds of plankton surfaceward—
pelagic constellations.

Squid follow, netting
radiant copepods,
their three hearts singing.
(*My four chambers thrilling.*)

Jennifer Harrison

The Giant Australian Cuttlefish

The giant Australian cuttlefish drifts in shallow ocean
        kelp fields fluttering along Antarctic tides—a flaneuse
she breeds where sharks deliver their oddly leathered eggs
and pumice from Chile washes ashore...

Inland from Adelaide the huge Olympic Dam has gouged out
450 kilometres of earth and ore—but here in the bay
madam propels herself away from nearer prey
(the bottle-nosed dolphin, a predator higher in the chain)...

She squirts an ink cloud that spreads like the veil
of a storybook widow we might read about in Dickens
or a fine romance, and how could she know that the defences
of her species have not kept pace with change?

The Port Bonython desalination plant would have tongued
        a pipeline through her seaweed world
but she knows nothing of CEOs, polished cedar tables
        conversations in taut boardrooms on the 35th floor

where Papunya paintings, vibrant as iridophores
hold her colours to the wall...She cannot drift
to higher ground and cannot fathom the futility
of her fierce inky protest—the plot is hashed online

where a web is spun by a giant insouciant spider...
        Giants are invisible of course—what do we know
of beanstalks? Always the boy climbing higher to win the bread
and beans? Uranium tailings leak 5000 tonnes per year

but she is a jewel of unpolished spinel...She mates with the great
southern currents, her progeny feeding on prawns, reef fish
and tommy roughs; queen of Point Lowly, she floats
diaphanously with her aunties in the middle of False Bay...

Matthea Harvey

My Octopus Orphan

thinks his suction cups are radios.
He presses them to his head and
it's always Ma playing on AM,
Father on FM. His eyes turn inward,
and he buries himself in the sand.
When the cephalopod sonogram
comes back, it shows his poison sac is
choc-a-block and leaking internally,
his ink sac predictably empty after
the hundreds of gloomy telegrams
with which he's muddied the walls
of his glass world. I know it's an aquarium
cliché, but I buy him a tricked-out
shipwreck from Goldfish Utopia.
Sometimes he squashes himself inside,
leaving only his hard beak on deck
and the only way to lure him out
is with his favorite snack of snails.
He sure knows how to look lonely.
Though I hold it in the water long
enough, he never takes my hand.
He understands: There was the sea, then me.

James Hoch

Polycardial

You don't have to be a cephalopod
to understand it's good to have a spare
hidden somewhere in the body's crags.
You don't need to possess random
superpowers nor free dive in arctic rifts
or play emotional whack-a-mole.
I mean, who couldn't use a wonderfully
engorged backup, a blue reliever
to answer the hunger of being human.
You never know. You never know.
But spares, these days, hard to come by.
Can't score them in the East Village
anymore, not dozing on a bench
in Tompkins Square Park, not even
Brooklyn. Forget Brooklyn. Imagine.
Some days you slump in the paunch
of a lawn chair, sipping gin and tonic,
and a Gremlin goes by and you dream
the smell of your teenage self and herself,
how you took time, how she showed you,
kissing in an orange beater that forever
faintly stunk of oil and singed carburetor
hose and stale Parliament cigarettes.
Her car, her mouth. It was good, right?
In your rush, you were kind, right?
All those fantasies are now memories.
They float in a softly lit aquarium
exhibit you've curated your whole life,
and you are almost returned to 1982
yellowy streetlamp night, cassettes
playing "Take on Me"…"I Melt with You"…
Why are we equal parts tender and not?

Perhaps, we were once polycardial:
one heart of air; the other air that burns.
Maybe one burst and cauterized
the other. Or the humans exhausted
all the feelings, so ran to the fjord
and threw our wasted heart into the sea.
Which might explain squid and octopi,
and why we are lousy at swimming,
and why your heart thaws in the sink
of your old tired weak worn-out body
which no longer sleeps, which wakes
and stirs the warm second you hear
your wife open the screen door
or children shrieking in the yard
as they gather jarfuls of fireflies.
Listen: Let the air be an ocean.
Let the ocean occupy your tongue.

Rebecca Hoogs

Pseudomorph

I feel like a Rebecca-
like shape, like the real one

has cast me off, spurt me out
and left me to face her predators,

like the real me is off
enjoying her airpocketless body,

while I stay behind going blotto,
a so-so blurb on the back of a book,

a blurry word. My beak keens
for something to say, but I'm a bubble

that's lost its thought, an ink-tank
without a think. O morph, o nym,

I'm know I'm just your pseudo,
your thin skin, but please

return my heart and other vitals.
It's thankless, this being*like*,

a being not quite right.

Shurouq Ibrahim

Pelagic

I once read that octopi usually live
in the deep oceans,
but some—I assume the cheeky ones—
are pelagic.
Pelagic;
I am not ashamed to admit
I had to look the word up.
Pelagic:
Living near the surface of the water.
Social butterflies, you may deem them.
These greedy cephalopods who found that
all of the ocean was not enough.
These beings who wanted more.
I am the opposite;
I wish to delve deep and wide,
avoid all things pelagic.
Or perhaps—
I am not the opposite.
Perhaps we are exactly the same.

Anissa Lynne Johnson

Mood Ring

The longer the giant Pacific octopus broods her eggs, the less potent her superpowers become. Refusal to leave her den for food renders her unable to self-heal from the white lesions covering her skin. Unable to shape-shift or ink or change colors and textures as camouflage, communication. A kaleidoscope of emotion in her chromatophore cells once made the octopus into an underwater mood ring. Dark colors for aggression. Pale colors for retreat and fear. Charcoal & crimson & violet. Blush & blonde & porcelain. But now, in the darkness of her rocky den, the octopus dons only ghastly gray. A premonition of her fate to come.

In the meantime, she fights the eternal exhaustion in her eight legs. The giant Pacific octopus' 56,000 eggs, hanging from the den's ceiling like bunches of grapes, need her. She blows jets of water over them with her siphon, providing the unborn baby octopuses with oxygen. Expels harmful bacteria and algae that like to feed on their egg casings.

This is the octopus' daily duty until hatching day, the soon-coming event keeping her tethered to this world despite waning strength.

After seven months of brooding, the hatchlings finally free themselves from their egg casings. Perfect miniatures of their parents the size of a grain of rice, already able to defend themselves by changing colors or releasing a tiny puff of ink at a predator. With her dying breath, the giant Pacific octopus blows her babies towards the surface, where they'll feed and grow. Fight their own battles against blue whales, jellyfish, and sharks. Of the 56,000 new lives, only two will reach adulthood.

But their mother doesn't know that for sure. She watches the
baby octopuses through her cloudy eyes until she can keep
them open no longer.

Clare Johnson

Post-it Note Project (excerpts)

haven't heard from you.
8/15/11

5.28.14
I'M
GOING
TO
THE
OCEAN,
eventually.

planned parenthood,
which might be
overlooked.
6.8.15

every time I see you in this shirt
it feels like
I've found my place in the world
all my places in the world
all my places are in the world somewhere
some things work out
3.27.16

Jen Karetnick

I Commiserate with the Pygmy Octopus Found in the Miami Beach Parking Garage

First time? I get it. In this place, it's inevitable
to cling to cement like forgotten spaghetti
in the bottom of the pot. Bottom dwellers, holders

of the smallest hopes, we have so much in common.
Always it's a rude awakening to find yourself flush
on the floor under the neon glare of a super beaver

moon, the surging sea a near distance, that uterine shed
of toxic algae, the sick-room stink sweeping in long
before the scarlet-feathered dawn, pushing you into

a place you never thought you'd go. All three of your
hearts were born to know what dying is, but this is
different: only air beats through your gills to replace

their copper charges. *Canary in the coalmine of climate
change,* marine biologists call you. *Expect more sea
creatures in dry spaces.* Twitter sends recipes, sarcasm.

*This is from the city that brought the world a shark
on the Metrorail. Is it running for mayor?* Harbinger
or hoax, but alive when security scoops you into a bucket

of saltwater and deposits you home—the question is not
how long can you survive out of the ocean, but why should
we have to see your blood to know how much bluer it runs?

But, Black, It Can't

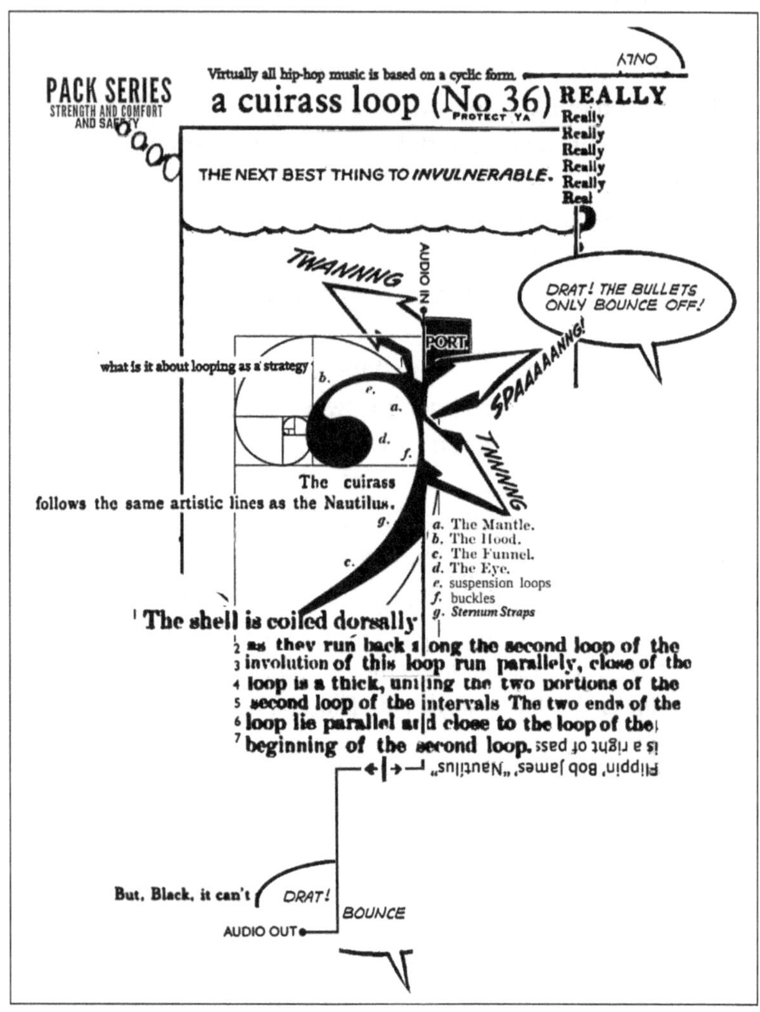

Donika Kelly

A Poem to Remind Myself of the Natural Order of Things

You are of a mind, a reiteration
along a different branch—our nearest,
shared relative: a flat worm.

You are in a jar, your tentacles both
of themselves and you, spinning the lid
from inside. O little octopus,

I am full of questions. How did this happen,
this laboratory, this maze, the lights
you short with a jet of water? Your camera's

eye, your hard beak, what you pulled
along the ocean floor to your burrow?
Where is the ocean? Who put you in the jar?

What have they taught you to settle for?
And what do they know of our several minds?

Richard Kenney

Eight Smart

Scene One:

Smart as a cat, the octopus unscrews the lid from the inside, slops
No drop, scooting to the roll-chair where the lab tech sprawls
    asleep,
Lifts his car keys, taps the eight-digit keypad code, clicks the lock,
And books it for the parking garage.

Scene Two:

                                    It's a good look:
Tesla-like, an elbow crooked out every window, photochromatic
    Ray-Bans
Adjusting to the sun—

Scene Three:

                    And now in the rear-view mirror, the blue light
    spins.
The cruiser swims aside. A good deal smarter than a cat, the
    octopus pulls over,
Keystrokes octuply quick on his i-phone, he hacks the police
    mainframe, proffers
A fresh identity:
He's a *Kennedy.*

Scene Four:

           Under police escort, smarter than we can imagine, the
    octopus steers
West, turning the color of a Turner-grade sunset, into which he
    disappears.

Rachel Kessler

Inky's Ghazal

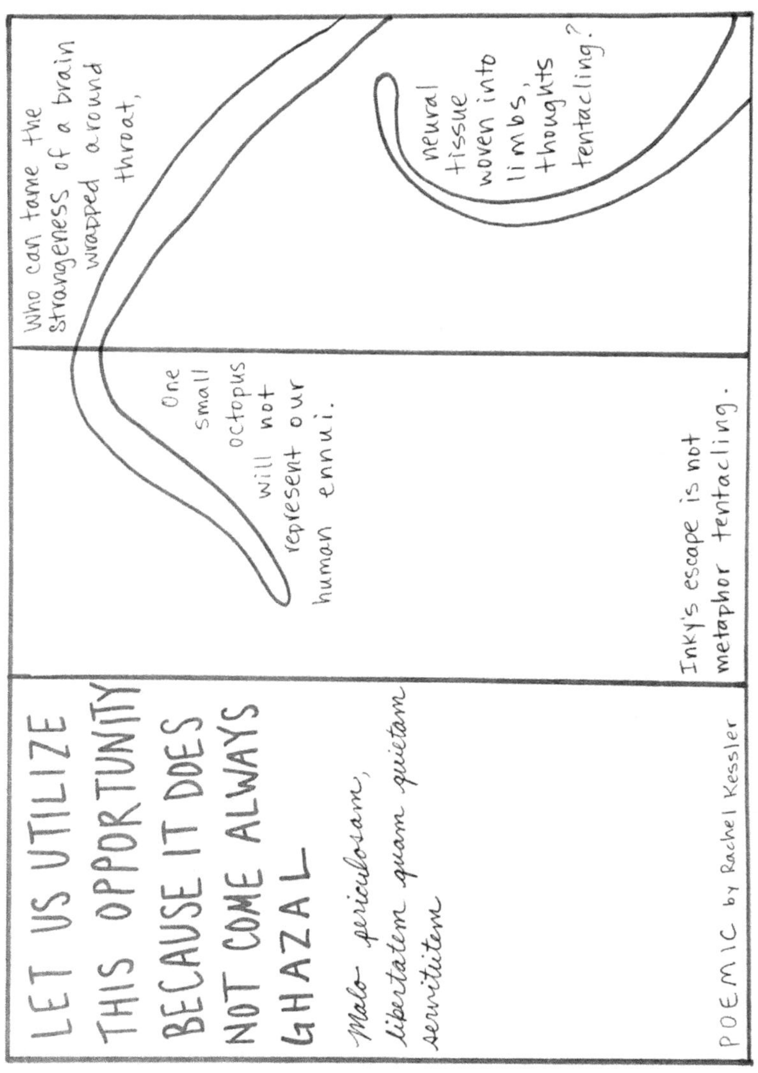

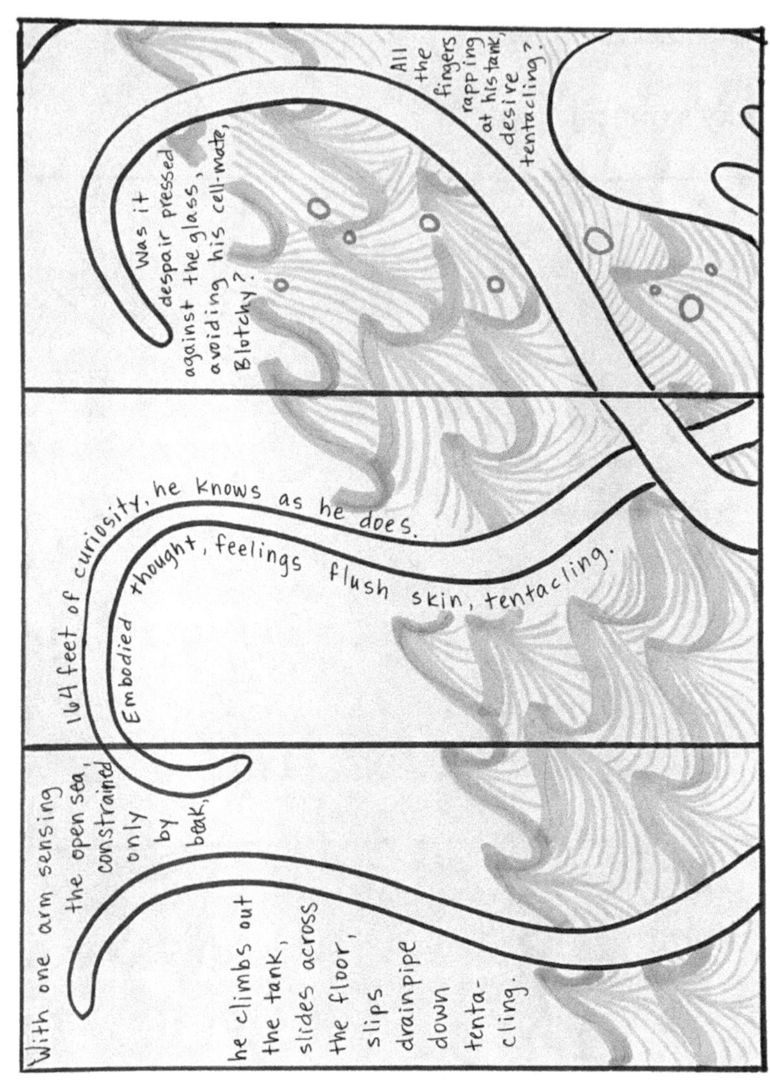
All the fingers rapping at his tank, desire tentacling?
Was it despair pressed against the glass, avoiding his cell-mate, Blotchy?
164 feet of curiosity, he knows as he does.
Embodied thought, feelings flush skin, tentacling.
With one arm sensing the open sea, constrained only by beak,
he climbs out the tank, slides across the floor, slips drainpipe down tenta-cling.

Maybe he did not run from. Maybe he moved to understand.
His mind maps the sea inside,
a freedom tentacling.
"If horses had hands
they would draw their gods
like horses."
Homer should've expressed himself in pulsing color flesh tentacles.
Wittgenstein said, like, don't anthropomorphize. Those aren't arms.
"if a lion could talk we could not understand him."

Rachel Kessler

What the Natural World Tells Us

When you take away the shell you have to think.
She had it, then she lost it.
Now a female squid carries her egg sac in her mouth—
9 months without eating.

When she zooms away from the camera,
a tail of single eggs trails
behind her, Hansel and Gretel-ing,
doomed. Like the breadcrusts,
the tiny gloves,
the handknit hats,
the scarves, the socks
I leave in my wake
when I am pushing the stroller.
When I am running the broom.
When I am running the broom across the floor.
When I am running the broom across the ocean floor—
Can you hear the tiny bubbles of my singing?

It is very easy to understand

the pair of children's underpants inside the piano.
What we jettison to survive.

No shell left.
I have to think.

Look at what we used to be:
elegant, oblivious paper nautilus.
Once we promenaded the ocean floor,

argonaut arms sailing.
100 flagellating limbs,
perfect and ancient and unthinking.

We carried our houses on our backs.

And this starving
is Evolution.

Sarah Key

The Parc Güell Octopus

I
Clings upside down in deep REM on the hypostyle ceiling.

II
Undulates with her brother the sea serpent. He pretends to
be the longest bench. On warm days she cools off in cousin
dragon's pool.

III
Tickles sleeping tourists in multi-armed attacks. She loves
French ladies who forget to close their mouths.

IV
Squeezes through the fence on weekdays to play chess with
school children next door, her pawns broken tea cups stolen
from the trencadís mosaics.

V
Shines all the crockery at night with her suckers. She
chromatomorphs to her favorite patterns, colors, textures. She
becomes chains of pink DNA, tie-dyed planets, Stars of David.
Men make her blush. She prefers not to change in front of
them.

VI
Photo-bombs large Japanese tour groups. They never find her
in the photo. Sometimes she gargoyles a lion.

VII
Interprets beak-to-beak for parrots who gossip with the throaty
old Catalan men. She dreamt they said Gaudí was beatified for
the miracle of vegetarianism.

VIII

Walks on her arms up to the three crosses. All three hearts
ablaze, she eight-waves to her friends in the far-off sea.

Sarah Key

Why I'd Rather Be a Teuthologist Than a Poet

Because I am the kind of girl
who cuddles with cuttlefish.

To shed the cost of ink and paper
and flow with water-writers.

To know how to beat
every line with three hearts.

Let my awry syntax go
grasp how to RNA-edit.

To banish villanelles, embrace the villainy
of Red Devils, the most disarming of squids!

To enjamb all my lines
cram my body in undersea crevices.

My metaphors cannot color
as fast as chromatophores.

Learn how the octopus sings in voltas
because my sonnets turn only once.

Personify with inky mucus
to pseudomorph my getaway.

Unlock the arm-waving
of octaves worm by worm.

Haikus will never be
cuter than bobtail squid.

Learn to rhyme with my bacteria—
let it light me bright as the moon.

Kathleen Kimball-Baker

Las Animas: Finding A Sea of Souls

> *A dream hangs over the whole region,*
> *a brooding kind of hallucination.*
>   — John Steinbeck, *The Log from the Sea of Cortez*

The only light: a slow whirl of stars.
Murmur of waves nearby; sleep comes easily.

I have come to the Sea of Cortez
         to put death aside for a week.

Night deepens and coyotes enter the dark camp.
They don't howl; they scream.

Threads of the canvas yurt collect their screams,
twine them into a bewilderment of dreams:

Once again I hold my mother
as her breathing slowly winnows from agonal to light
to gone.

At sunrise, I track paw prints on the shore, but
I find no coyotes, no scat. I find something else,
something big and brooding. Something beached.
My legs fold beneath me,
and I kneel beside a squid,
run my hands along
its alien skin. The muscle
of its body swells,
round and taut, as if
inhaling the desert's
air, as if holding

its breath, as
if unsure what
comes next—

release.
Around me on the beach, women
tip their heads into an arch
above us. Someone breaks
the long silence:

—*I think it's gone, honey.*

The only sound: waves.
The only sight: cool gray body beneath my palms.
The only feel: a slow recessional of tides.
The camp guide, once a soldier, pulls
the squid into the sparkling surf,
and with his machete, he slices away
long flowing limbs, holds up
the predatory beak: a trophy.

For dinner
the village women offer us:
calamari.

Morning.
A fishing boat motors
us toward familiar.
Wind whips my hair,
wets my lips with brine.

I close my eyes
and I see his strange skin—
where I touch him:

luminous prints of my hands,
sequins of words
flickering, a ship's wake under starlight.

Tara King

Seeing

There's nothing to prepare you for seeing
An octopus, nine brains walking
Along a red, lumpy outcrop of reef,
As you watch, starfished, from
Above. Nothing
To prepare you for the sea water
You'll suck down your snorkel
When the octopus vanishes,
Skin rippling to become
That red, lumpy outcrop of reef.
Too, nothing to prepare you for the envy,
Indistinguishable from knocking, ceaseless waves,
as you float, a corpse unchanging,
Above the red, lumpy outcrop:
Why can't you become something else?

Susan Landgraf

Devil Fish in a Workshop with Second Graders

See the devil fish roll out its tentacles—
an arm with suction cups—a tongue
searching for crab. See its eyes
high on its nose looking around among

jellyfish, salmon, eels and whales
in the Pacific, talking to others of its kind
from pinks to browns to blues
because even though they're color blind

they show what they feel with their colors.
Notice how each arm can go
its independent way, one backwards,
another up or down in that inky black cold

of the great sea where they rise out of waves
like eight-armed ghosts that never sleep,
that keep storytellers busy writing words
about octopuses living in the deep.

Katherine Larson

Love at Thirty-Two Degrees

I

Today I dissected a squid,
the late acacia tossing its pollen
across the black of the lab bench.
In a few months the maples
will be bleeding. That was the thing:
there was no blood
only textures of gills folded like satin,
suction cups like planets in rows. *Be careful
not to cut your finger*, he says. But I'm thinking
of fingertips on my lover's neck
last June. Amazing, hearts.
This branchial heart. After class,
I stole one from the formaldehyde
and watched it bloom in my bathroom sink
between the cubes of ice.

II

Last night I threw my lab coat in the fire
and drove all night through the Arizona desert
with a thermos full of silver tequila.

It was the last of what we bought
on our way back from Guadalajara—
desert wind in the mouth, your mother's
beat-up Honda, agaves
twisting up from the soil
like the limbs of cephalopods.

Parked outside of Tucson, saguaros so lovely
considering the cold, and the fact that you
weren't there to warm me.
Suddenly drunk I was shouting that I wanted to see the stars
as my ancestors used to see them—

To see the godawful blue as Aurvandil's frostbitten toe.

III

Then, there is the astronomer's wife
ascending stairs to her bed.

The astronomer gazes out,
one eye at a time,

to a sky that expands
even as it falls apart

like a paper boat dissolving in bilge.
Furious, fuming stars.

When his migraine builds and
lodges its dark anchor behind

the eyes, he fastens the wooden buttons
of his jacket, and walks

outside with a flashlight
to keep company with the barn owl

who stares back at him with eyes
that are no greater or less than

a spiral galaxy.
The snow outside

is white and quiet
as a woman's slip

against cracked floorboards.
So he walks to the house

inflamed by moonlight, and slips
into the bed with his wife

her hair and arms all
in disarray

like fish confused by waves.

IV

Science—

beyond pheromones, hormones, aesthetics of bone,
every time I make love for love's sake alone,

I betray you.

David Lasky

SQUID TANKA

Irene Latham

To an Octopus That's Lost an Arm

That ache you feel
is no phantom—
you will never
be the same.

But even now
new cells are swelling.
Swaddle yourself
in kind currents,
let time
do its work.

Each tide brings
you closer
to your potential.
Each moment
you become
       more.

Brett Fletcher Lauer

How the World Ends

Mostly I'm alone, ill-
omened, once called

a monster. I'm slow
at processing my feelings

of forgiveness. A head
devoid of all appendages,

except spite, primarily
for the Scandinavian

myths and Alfred, Lord
Tennyson's poem

"The Kraken" in which
he anticipates the ocean

waters warming and
erasing the coast of Miami

causing some beast of his
imagination to float

from the muck of abysmal
depths, decaying plant

stuff, and absent daylight,
up to the sea's surface

in a final death patrol.
It won't be fire and it's

not ice—the world ends
with me, what Victor

Hugo described as a terrible
masterpiece, or "glue

filled hatred" and so
my oversized tentacles

surround a ship. No,
I don't believe in vengeance

or a gusto to manifest
Tennyson's thesis,

something altogether
different, more akin

to the Prince of Thieves
or Bernie Madoff, the riches

returned to darkness,
to myth, to my sea cave—

a rusted-out oil drum
walls covered with paintings,

the tentacle used as a stencil
a dark cloud of ink sprayed

leaving just a silhouette,
to mark that I was there.

Emily Lawson

Aubade with Deep Sea Footage

Do you know about the blanket octopus? If we met while I had cancer,
I made you watch the video. Among us somewhere in the galactic
black. First, pale in the cruel beam of the submersible, her head
glows bulbous, like blown glass—then wings swoop out to drop the
shimmering mantle, unfurling, falling silk, slow-motion arabesque
in spectral pastel—*can you believe this?*—like a hex cast, or a chant
sung through the gloom. Trailing yards of filmy gossamer, a
bubble's swirling membrane. Wielding, as weapons, as whips,
tentacles ripped from a Portuguese Man O' War. Think of that.
Hovering like a Venusian spacecraft. How can I begin to say what
it meant to me? That I had gone so long without knowing. That
she was not washed ashore somewhere, deflated, gelatinous, a
wet plastic bag—not this one—but soaring, a living aurora. And
here on Earth, where I slept and vomited. That childhood's magic
rippled, rare and luminous, through that footage. Lighting my
cadaverous face. This morning, in remission, I woke from the
vision I had memorized, then forgotten, knowing I might choose
it, if I could, as my last: *actual alien, actual angel,* the color of sunrise,
of morphine, dream worlds, melting absinthe, orchids, lip gloss,
innards, gumdrops, moonstones, oil slicks: this nebula warping
through the infinite underworld—a kind of breathing, a kind of
weeping—flung untouchable satin, seraphic, labial, ethereal. Just
to live to see you,
O phantom, O weird mysterium—it's enough.

Donna J. Gelagotis Lee

Octopus on a Clothesline

<pre>
                    I
                can't quite
              shake the vision
            of the octopus hanging
             from the clothesline
             beside the towels and
            the crisp sun-dried linens,
             trouser legs, and shirt arms
       dangling   and find   sauce a
       like the arms the sweet woman makes
     of the octopus, female   with olives
        limp, clean as freed   I could   beside
        day can be,   rather   have picked   the
         the long   than   but did not   coast,
        appendages   pinned   every   the
         drying,   today   fall on   waters
         if only   before   hillsides   of
         I could   lying   covered   her
          look   in   with   own
          again   wine   olives   home
</pre>

Jill Leininger

Squid Babies, Born Like Stars

Birth is not a picnic, but you have to imagine
something. You're just laying out
the blanket now. Rest.

When the time comes, take it at your waist
and shake whatever remains of
your once too ample lunch,

crumbs and strawberry seeds scattered
to the wind. YouTube and the giant squid
will teach you all you need to know.

And although her dance does not resemble
the jerk and turns that it will take
to get you to your feet, nor any of
your desperate practice

at the toilet—all the Kegels, and that drip-
shimmy you learned in the woods—
you are bound to get a little wet.

The weight of it will bring you as close
as you've ever been to the earth
repeatedly. But you will not die.

So rest. Like the squid,
you will only do this once:

the chromophores and half-notes
falling; one of your giant eyes

watching a thousand
possibilities detach to sink deeper
and brighter into the cold which now
belongs more to them;

the other eye
trained on the sun
and filtering the water's surface
into small, unresolved harmonies.

That counter-urge and counterpoint
is only the first movement
of the song that will tear you apart.

Priscilla Long

Tarot Spread: Divination

I'm blindfolded, blind
to a past I cannot see.
I stoop—fieldhand,
peasant bearing stones,
rootwads, stumps.
But wishing to fly,
wishing to sing, wishing
to sink into oceans
strange with sea-urchins,
or that unctuous orange
octopus. Wishing to swim,
I'm let to swim,
guided into deeps,
lifted by some fishy muse
into lightness and light.

Oscar Lortz (composed at age 7)

Cuttlefish (A Sonnet)

Cuttlefish are cool
Cuttlefish live in a pool
Cuttlefish need water to survive
They migrate in an underwater hive

Cuttlefish are very smart
Cuttlefish are natural art
Cuttlefish squirt dark clouds of ink
They are a natural sink

Cuttlefish are a big surprise
Cuttlefish are masters of disguise
Cuttlefish are not mammals
They are one amazing animal

Cuttlefish eat crabs
Cuttlefish have really hard grabs!

Pat Lowther

Octopus

The octopus is beautifully
functional as an umbrella;
at rest a bag of rucked skin
sags like an empty scrotum
his jelled eyes sad and bored

but taking flight: look
how lovely purposeful
in every part:
the jet vent smooth
as modern plumbing
the webbed pinwheel of tentacles
moving in perfect accord
like a machine dreamed
by Leonardo

Julie Maclean

Emily Dickinson as an Octopus with a Pre-Death Plan

*I'm afraid I can't explain myself, sir. Because I am not
myself, you see?*
      —Lewis Carroll, *Alice's Adventures Underground.*

From the high-care low-life facility where my head lolls in the
briny bowl Doctor Death asks what my priorities are What
goals i have in the short term What i am prepared to sacrifice
What not   I'll tell you what   I want to make bad choices—
pick a fight, drink red wine, raid the fridge at midnight, steal
that woman's earrings, disembowel carnations, rip to shreds
that New Idea then shoot for a wave where an octopus looks me
in the eye like a Hindu god with the wisdom of a newborn babe,
takes my measure, shows me personality, holds a tea party with
nothing in it but chocolate cake and opioids then hides me in
her cave, the two of us minus our ancestral shells sharing a
spliff, smoking our guffawing heads off

Back in the tank outside visiting hours we are chastened and
when nobody's looking she oozes across to greet me in redness
of excitement   i touch her head, she turns creamy white,
relaxed like no one i know, so many lobes coil around her
throat, she meets my mind, spits salt water in my face to show
me how much she knows me, she knows me, bored to death by
melancholy squeezing her boneless body through aquarium
bars it's mayhem as she marches across her Amherst lawn
suckering everything in her path *Down down down* to the water
changing colour pattern texture spots commas, slashing pages
with short lines-long-necked, funny, unlived Emily playing
with rage and form, dying tired without me, alone

Kika Man 文詠玲

Octopus turned inside out

I was so sad that I was happy.
Actually, it was my happiness that made the tides swell.
Melancholy grew to the size of a banana tree,
an octopus turned inside out.

Kindra McDonald

I Fell in Love with a Cephalopod

A brief squid who swam into my palm
when I needed it, standing chest deep
in the Chesapeake in a lightning storm
lost and empty, bobbing along between
end and start over, asking the sky for a sign
rocking in the brackish heart of the bay
and she slipped in my cupped hand
her eye was my eye and she saw all
I'd been and could be and stayed—
head foot, all arms and my own salt heart
beating alive, yes, this is what it means
to love even your wrecked self, translucent
and raw.

Linda Mitchell

haiku Found in *A Handbook to the National Museum* 1886

1.
octopus limbs
grasp, enfold and draw in prey
of squid proportions

2.
dimensions
are valuable in the
cold fiords

Linda Mitchell

Middle School Octopus

from Octopus focus on key features for camouflage

The first day of seventh-grade is about **camouflage**.
Don't do anything to be seen or heard. It **is**
the deadliest whirlpool of your life. If you **used**
brilliance to survive elementary school, drop it. Better **to**
blend in with cephalopods, move along with suckers—be a **fool**
swimming, eating, inking, like the others. **A**
fish in the center of a school isn't tempting prey. **Wider**
expectations for success must be met out of **range**
of waking hormones and lab partners, projects, square-dancing... **of**
growing undetected, passed over by bigger teen **predators**.

Ruth Mota

The Octopus

Bless mother octopus.
Cephalopod of languid arms that taste
and open to the third unsuccored tentacle of love.
Embrace his sperm, embrace his last gift
wrap it safely near the hidden beak.
Watch arms swirl in an alluring dance.
Like diaphanous crimson scarves they beckon,
then, in a flash, transform
to pebbled patterns of the rocks below—
red to checkered gray.
Be here. Be nowhere.
Father's life force gone, she
pumps blue blood from her three hearts,
nourishes and waits
for more mates to fertilize before she
glides into her cave,
weaves a chandelier of spider lights, before she
blows last breaths away to tend her hanging brood.
Watch life leave her as it blossoms on her roof.
She starves herself for the few
who will survive
the dangers of our dying sea.

Shankar Naryan

Love Letter from Immigrant to Octopus

We are impossible creatures
five octopus lifetimes into this country, impossible

to unfamiliar tongues—enter—
octopus dofleini, Shankar Rajamani. Enter, god

with infinite arms, mesmerize past
ironic borders to America's dark

waters where we den and hide from ice-
cold predators, eyes huge and omnivorous for things just

beyond our grasping, stealing colors
of our captors. We are lovers loving to death,

then feeding our bodies to each other, to something beyond
our lives, like your parents working sweat-

shop jobs for so many lifetimes
for the small miracle of you. Sacrifice the body

and move on. Master your disguise, ink
wisely, obfuscate when necessary

to survive, curiosity immune
to catastrophe. How can we be still

when the wild world beckons just
beyond that glass border? Octopus, I feel

the art of your escape, unstoppable
no matter how small the opening, compress the mortal

body to the size of a hungry mouth—
the only solid thing you own—swallow the pulse

and go. This is what freedom
is—taste its eightfold embrace, dozens of suckers,

thousands of hooks, meaning hang onto what you love
with everything you've got. And when what you love

is a distant sea the grey skies keep drizzling into—
remember all oceans are yours

and the limb you dip in the Duwamish
is already touching Mumbai. In the end, become our own

parachutes unfurling into a Milky Way
of inconceivable appendages, defy the odds

and thrive, dwarf to world-swallowing god
in three paces. Nurture our hidden weapons—the poison

turning blue rings in your throat, a secret apocalypse
to be unleashed with divine grace, a dance that ignites

the cosmos. Open
your arms, leave them all stunned. Touch

the vein just under the skin
of your white lover's wrist, already turning colors

you've never seen. Feel her blood pulse
blue. Feel coral borders, galaxies collapsing. Who knew this
        consuming

would be so beautiful? In this country everyone grasps
royalty but only you

have three hearts—one
for here, one

for elsewhere, and one
for the world beyond glass

in which you
will never be whole.

Jane Wandel Nelson

Being the Cuttlefish

Not from an act of central will
directed by a vision
but from the skin itself
all those chromatophores
yellow over blue and red
then brown and black beneath
but lower still iridophores
reflect metallic blue and green
and gold and silver—Ah!
Complexity of adaptation
layer upon layer
like a life of secrets
only gradually revealed
to one's Self

Sierra Nelson

Cephalopod Meditation

*Inspired by the slides of Dr. Roland C. Anderson (1947-2014), the
Seattle Aquarium's renowned octopus expert and longtime friend
of the Cephalopod Appreciation Society.*

How long have you been hiding from yourself?

Coiling inward protectively, squishing yourself into
convenient, hard shapes?

When they didn't understand how you saw things,
did you start to see yourself as they thought you were?

Did you forget you could see with more than just the eye?
Your whole skin sensing flashes of light and passing shadow,
giving and receiving colors like touch?

What other parts have you forgotten,
still breathing inside of you?

What vulnerable underside
is quivering its suction cups?

Was this even one of your three hearts?

How many tears cried, and on what scale?

What can you discover in what's been discarded:
the midden of your past, abandoned shells and carapace?

And what have you been clinging to, afraid to let go?

Desire moves, all muscle, with sinuous strength.

Did you fear you were some kind of monster?
Did somebody call you that?

Are you trying to keep it all under control?
And how is that going?

Have you come to the far edge of the life you've known so far—
sensing something in yourself beyond the cold glass?

Have you been trying to communicate,
by chromatophore and gesture,
the awkward, beautiful, futile, dance of it?

Is it all a dance?
[*dance*]
[*dance*]

And what about love?
Had you found it before?
Did you make a map to try to find it again?

We are only here such a short time,
before interrupted by illness, accident,
or subsiding into pale senescence.

What if these moments are your last?
What are you thinking? Making?
Who are you caring for?

What are you tending now to send into the future?
What words, what images, what hope—
tucked into small fragile vessels like messages in a bottle,
growing their own chromatophores, secret signals?

And how will you be remembered?

Lesléa Newman

Arms Race

I can write a ten-page letter
While I mend my favorite sweater,
Drive a tractor, bake a cake,
Gather up some leaves to rake,
Play some songs on my guitar,
Brush my teeth and wash my car.
I do this with no muss or fuss
Because I am an octopus.

Aimee Nezhukumatathil

Invitation

Come in, come in. The water's fine! You can't get lost
here. Even if you want to hide behind a clutch
      of spiny oysters—I'll find you. If you ever leave me
     at night, by boat, you'll see the arrangement

of red-gold sun stars in a sea of milk. And though
it's tempting to visit them—stay. I've been trained
      to gaze up all my life, no matter the rumble
     on earth, but I learned it's okay to glance down

into the sea. So many lessons bubble up if you know
where to look. Clouds of plankton churning
      in open whale mouths might send you east
     and chewy urchins will slide you west. Squid know

how to be rich when you have ten empty arms.
Can you believe there are humans who don't value
      the feel of a good bite and embrace at least once a day?
     Underneath you, narwhals spin upside down

while their singular tooth needles you
like a compass pointed towards home. If you dive
      deep enough where imperial volutes and hatchetfish
     swim, you will find all the colors humans have not yet

named, and wide caves of black coral and clamshell.
A giant squid finally let itself be captured
      in a photograph, and the paper nautilus ripple-flashes
     scarlet and two kinds of violet when it silvers you near.

Who knows what will happen next? And if you still want
to look up, I hope you see the dark sky as oceanic—
     boundless, limitless—like all the shades of blue in a glacier.
     Listen how this planet spins with so much fin, wing, and fur.

Katherine Ogle

Aquarium

A jellyfish floats the ocean hallway
like a plastic bag on a breeze.

From the way it dances to the music,
you might say it is having a good time.

I had a good time once.

I was weightless in the Aegean,
convinced I was a mermaid
when a fish bit me on the toe.

I then remembered I was no part fish, or
only fish in the historical sense.

We walk into the turtle theater
as a head of lettuce drops
into the top of the tank.
The loggerbacks make their way.

Head-foot. Ink-fish.
In the cephalopod room,
I am getting used to the idea
that I know very little.
You're allowed to eat soft-serve here.

A guide demonstrates the squid's locomotion
by drawing her fingers together and swooping along.
Mantle, siphon, tentacles. She leaves the room this way.

I believe my son is too young
to know how to play dead,

and yet there he is on the carpet,
prone before the only mollusks that bleed.

I guide him to a sink.
We wash our hands for the touch tank.

In the sea, life began again and again until it took.

Shin Yu Pai

Gyotaku

The passengers aboard our Puget Sound bound vessel included a bespoke shoemaker, a floral designer, and two lawyers. A group of strangers had assembled together on a rainy winter night to experience squid jigging. I was standing beside Evan, a retired smokejumper, when he pulled the juvenile squid out of the Salish Sea. Our marine biologist-in-residence for the night came over to examine the freshly caught specimen.

I felt a terrible sense of responsibility for this animal's life—it had been preparing to spawn when the lighted lures hanging off our barge attracted him to swim towards our vessel. The opalescent animal met my gaze with an unblinking, silent stare. As the scientist prodded the miniature squid, he released a spurt of black ink that stained the creases of Evan's weathered palm.

My professional work puts me in a position to design and produce uncommon experiences for people. My friend David had come to me with the idea of organizing a squid fishing expedition that could celebrate a unique Pacific Northwest tradition—a migration that can be seen late at night along the piers of Elliott Bay and West Seattle throughout late Fall and early Winter.

The eerie beauty of the luminescent lures and fishing lines of squid jiggers rivals only the magic of walking into low tide at midnight to encounter hundreds of razor clam diggers outfitted in headlamps as they overturn sand along the shoreline. These romantic images filled my imagination when I agreed to produce the event and chartered a private boat. But I came late to realizing the horror of what we were actually planning: A hunting expedition where kinship with nature would mean taking a life.

I am a Buddhist. I'd taken vows to do no harm. To respect all life and to honor all sentient beings.

David pulled out a sheet of fine art Strathmore and spread the squid's figure over the textured white paper, so that the guests on the boat could examine it more closely beneath a bright light. As the group gathered around the limp squid, the marine biologist scraped a plastic fork across its body to activate a rainbow of chromatophores.

I felt myself in the active act of breaking a vow. I had violated a commitment. And not only did I feel a profound disconnection to nature, I felt aware of being cut off from my own humanity.

"Does it feel pain?" someone asked.

"Does it understand what's happening to it?"

The scientist was diplomatic when he declared, "They have very highly developed sensory systems."

I was blinded by the tears filling my eyes and walked towards the back of the boat, where I could quietly weep unnoticed, as the biologist continued lecturing on cephalopod biology. I'd dreaded this moment the entire night and quietly prayed that we'd fail at our expedition.

That moment of gazing into the eyes of a dying squid was my personal turning of the wheel. Prince Siddartha touched it when he walked out beyond the palace walls to see a freshly plowed field that exposed the earthworms who made their homes there. The worms wriggled in distress trying desperately to find cover, while others writhed in pain having just been cleaved in two. All beings suffer. But in this instance, I contributed to creating suffering for another soul.

These events weigh upon me still. So often communion with nature involves the sublime, some experience of obliteration. In my ill-fated fishing expedition, it included an enactment of power upon a being whose life was perceived as lesser. We were wrong. I was wrong. No life has more value over another.

As the squid expired, someone bagged it and threw it into a plastic cooler. What remained was a natural imprint of the animal's body left behind on paper, in the tradition of a Japanese gyotaku or fish print—a record of the night's catch. In another print, drips of opalescent squid ink shimmer with gold. When I look at this image, I think of kintsugi, shattered ceramics that are carefully mended with a lacquer resin mixed with powdered gold. Ruptures and mending are part of the history. The damage is visible—and still somehow unspeakable in its beauty.

Pattie Palmer-Baker

Giant Pacific Octopus at the Hatfield Marine Science Center

I wait.

                  So long I have been waiting.

For a land-being to free me
from this caged aloneness.
Little do I care that they are sizeable tubes,
       lumpy
        with two
        uncurved stalk-
       like arms stuck
        to her sides
        and two for
     standing on   the outside
of this sea-water-filled, hard-air barriered,
see-through prison.

Not like me,
with eight arms to
    curl
       swirl
           spiral
      curve
    arc.

You land-beings on the other side of the barrier
with those bulbous white, blue or brown
circle-centered eyes,
can see my majesty.
Yes, you,
who spread your fibrous fingers

on the surface where I splay my body.
What do you want?
          Not that I care.

          Indifference stains my body pale.

I wait.
                    Then.
                         Above me!
                                   In a flesh-colored
                                                  flash
                         she appears.
She is unlike the other tubes.
She sees who I am.

I blaze crimson, unfurl two
of my arms to shoot out of the water,
bracelet
her
    wrists
          (without squeezing),
stroke the shelled crab she offers,
fold it in my second arm's efficient circle,
place it in my mouth politely, never greedily.

She tosses me colored balls.
The big yellow one, my favorite, I loop
into my sixth arm. My eighth arm
curls around the red ball and swishes
it toward my mouth's opening.
An octopus joke,
I won't eat it.

I long to wind
all eight arms around her torso,
pull her in to be my playmate, my friend

for
all of
the time.

No, what I really want—
to envelope her in my arms' soft spiral
until after dark. We can escape
to the boundaryless ocean.
I will protect her.
From orcas, sharks, moray eels.
Anything, everything.
I will squirt a black ink curtain
to hide her, or cover
her body with mine,
quick-changed
to look like a sea-boulder.

I know, I know, she cannot breathe the seawater.
And, although
I might be able to drag myself out,
the hard air stutters and slices
through my gills
and I slide-stick
on the unyielding surface.

You might not know this.
I have three
hearts.
Necessary to pump copper-rich blood
to my
supple
muscular arms.

Three hearts that can break.

Alixen Pham

The Three Chambers of Fatalism

How can we endure, knowing you don't recall
my body, a shifting blanket diaphanous as grief,

    drifting in slow mourning.

After you cleaved my heart into three, the ocean
nautiluses my flesh into a spiraling procession

    of shrinking funerals.

I tuck memories into eight arms,
haunting the spaces between your fingers.

    My touch parrots you black

and yellow. Your hands lift my mantle, a cape
iridescent as a nebula of stars.

    Do you see me now with your pelagic eye?

My crown bleached coral, echoes of Orpheus
on black sandy islands where my voice inks

    despair on seaweed testaments.

Who prays here now?
Who waters salt from our eyes?

    A chorus of sea urchins with hearts of teeth?

Your mouth beaks red from my belly.
A tide of my limbs begs the aphotic zone:

Return my shell to me.

Lisa Usani Phillips

Uncommon

I resolve to grow wings
strong enough to bear
my glory, unmitigated
by silks or any other
raiment whatsoever.

My bumps
shall hereby become sentient
my skin scrim and semaphore
my legs besuckered
all my limbs a tongue

tasting shell and rock
root, trunk, and branch
never mind the wind
I ascend
unfettered by breath
unfelled by fear
of beak or claw.

The clouds
will not satisfy.
I expel them
and thus escape
the few bounds left me.

Even longevity
may be mine
for an eye.

Verandah Porche

The Kraken Talks Back

Why dub me "monster" when we've never met?
The sea you call "abysmal" is my home.
O, Tennyson, I'm not some mammoth pet
your puny pen concocted for a poem.

I am alive, an island, one of a kind,
full fathoms five below the churning deep
where ancient currents seldom end in sleep,
though dark as ink and every eye is blind.

You think me mum or dumb and numb to all
the creatures nestled in my tentacles.
They scurry here for shelter when I call,
"A storm, a squall, a trawling fishing net!
Stay safe beneath my shifting silhouette."
No one with my looks could kill a soul.
I'm *She*, the sea's own Tree of Life, a miracle.

Rena Priest

Shimmy at the Volta

I.

Is it comforting to be told
that we are not alone?
Do you assume
whatever is with us
loves us?

Perhaps the being who
is busy conjuring clouds
is watching over us now.

II.

Does it unsettle you to be told
that we are not alone?
Are you made leery
by a lack of backstory?
Who's out there?

Perhaps intelligent aliens
with boney eyelids and
starlit iridescent eyes stare.

III.

Of course, we are not alone.
We have our own
strange reflections,
like wings of glass fluttering
in a maze of mirrors,

perhaps evolved to crack
so we can embark,
make breakthroughs.

IV.

We are alone if you believe
the universe is one big thing,
which it is—in the same way
an octopus has one big brain
and another in each leg.

Perhaps we are alone.
Shall we move joyfully and see
if anyone joins to have a shimmy?

V.

At the volta, have a shimmy
and another in each leg.
Make breakthroughs.

In a maze of mirrors, eyes stare.
Who's in there watching us?
Does it love us?

Labyrinthitis

Two children spin on a path in the woods.

○

Sometimes I think of spinning and the spinning starts.

○

Sometimes I think of you and the spinning starts.

○

When the muni train hit my car, I spun across the road and hit my head. This is when I blacked out. This is when the other spinning started.

○

I lie still on the table like a bug pinned to a mat while the doctor sticks his needles into my body. To stop the spinning. To keep the spinning stopped.

○

What is vertigo? asks somebody. It is Labrynthitis, I say, which is what the doctor said. What is labyrinthitis? I ask the doctor. It is the spinning, he says.

○

I walk through airports that never end
in flight and ride bicycles in circles
and worry about what I am leaving
behind.

$\circlearrowright$

And yes, I am aware that the mind is
inside the body and the vestibular
system is inside the head and the
brain is inside the mind and the body
is inside the universe and everything
and everyone everywhere is always
spinning.

$\circlearrowright$

What is vertigo? asks Milan Kundera.
It is the voice of the emptiness below

$\circlearrowright$

Sometimes I wonder if I spent too
many years trying to live too many
lives simultaneously.

$\circlearrowright$

After a hike, I lay on my bed beneath
a twenty five pound weighted blanket.
I closed the door. I closed the blinds. I
closed my eyes.

$\circlearrowright$

I float.

$\circlearrowright$

A room full of feathers, full of loft. All pillows and softness and white. There is no up. No down. No fear of falling. No fear of the voice of the emptiness below.

No fear of the emptiness below. The octopuses crawl along the shore for their nightly pilgrimage from the ocean to no one knows where. Or why.

Linda Neal Reising

Scuttlebutt from a Cuttlefish

Why should it surprise you that I can pass
the "marshmallow test," even when no spongy
confectionary is involved? My brain is the envy
of the sea, and my pupils are shaped like "W's"
for "Wonderment." And don't even get me started
on the pigment I can release—sepia—yes, Crayola
stole that from me. So, of course, I could play along
with the scientists who utilized two test chambers—
a piddly piece of king prawn in one, a luscious live
grass shrimp in the other. They didn't think
I could think well enough to control my desires,
but I am the duke of delayed gratification. I even gave
the crows and parrots a lesson in learning to wait.
For eons, my kind, camouflaged to match sea rock
or sand, have sat and waited for our prey, changing
colors so quickly, the doomed are shell-shocked,
hypnotized. Breaking stillness, our eight arms
shoot two long tentacles, grabbing, pulling to beaks,
paralyzing the stunned crabs or worms before feeding.
And don't be horrified to know that sometimes,
if the hunger is too great, we don't hesitate
to devour our own.

Linda Neal Reising

Taking Leave

> *Off he went. Didn't even leave us a message.*
> > —Rob Yarrell from the National Aquarium of
> > New Zealand, commenting on the escape of
> > Inky, the octopus.

How long did he plot the escape,
etching upon aquarium glass, Roman
numerals only he could see—one
tentacle touch for each day of the years
since a fisherman trapped him inside
a crayfish pot—counting every moon
cycle, tide swell, he missed. Inside
his cranium, he must have mulled
the possibility, his cephalopod brain
churning, forming a mental map,
waiting for one mistake, a gaffe, a gap
at the tank's top. And how his three
hearts must have beaten when at last
he saw his chance. Blue blood pulsing,
he contorted his way through, slid down
the side, a desert of concrete spread
before him. Limbs becoming legs,
he crossed to the drain pipe leading
into Hawke's Bay. And at that moment
of leaving, he knew what he must do—
draw inside himself, become so small,
lose the form he'd come to know
if he ever wished to once again
hold the sea's immensity in his arms.

Neil Rhind

Envoy From Fairyland

Blue-blooded changeling
Shifting shape
To blithely ape
The mundane world around her.

Frustrate her feigning
And she'll shroud
Herself in clouds
And vanish once you've found her.

Where there's a crack in
Two worlds' walls
Be it so small
She'll have space to slip between,

An unleashed Kraken.
Known to us
As Octopus
Though skeely as the Faery Queen.

Kim Roberts

Made From Darkness

> *"You octopi my thoughts"*
> —T.M.

The octopus is colorblind.
Yet its skin cells match the exact shade
of its environment, to blend into
rock, sand, or coral.
How do its cells know
what it cannot see? I saw
a film of a sleeping octopus
that changed colors rapidly

from pale ash-blue to piebald
to velvety black. Scientists
think it was dreaming.
On cave walls our earliest forbears
outlined the edges of animals
in ebony lines drawn with great economy
and rhythm, in manganese dioxide
mixed with grease.

The ancient Egyptians
made a pitch they called
km. Was it pronounced like my name?
A pigment made from burnt wood,
km was matte, the color
of the fertile mud of the Nile,
which was also called *km*.
You can find the octopus motif

on pot after pot crafted
by the Mycenaeans, its sable

sinuous tentacles curved
to the edges of ochre clay dishes
or wrapped around alabastrons,
large squat jars
where unguents were stored.
Two eyes like coals stare from a head

shaped like a figure eight,
the arms arrayed in impossible loops.
Tintoretto believed *the most beautiful
of all colors is black,* and Matisse
claimed *Black is a force.* Plato
explained vision as a ray of light
projected from our eyes.
Black objects spring into sight

from the narrowest type of ray
our eyes produce and taste,
he said, bitter on the tongue.
We now know, we have measured,
that it takes a ray of sunlight
eight minutes and twenty seconds
to reach earth, that long to cross
the concrete lip and climb my back stairs.

All of us live in the past.
Atramentum, a Latin term for black paint,
could be made three ways:
from the skin of grapes, dried
and left to calcify in the sun;
from burned ivory; and from the ink
of squid and cuttlefish,
varnished with gum arabic.

Gretchen Rockwell

Colossal Squid

I am almost rumor.
Shy, demure, I will not
surface to be seen for
your pleasure. I am not

the creature you think
you know, the kraken
cracking ship from stem
to stern. Instead, I am

elusive, fluid—a being
of light. Enormous eyes,
sharp beak, so bright
I blush at my own glory.

Gretchen Rockwell

Nautilus

My body is many rooms,
all nacreous and knife-thin.
I spiral marvelous, miraculous
through life, sealing off old selves
as I outgrow them. I stay cryptic—
camouflaged, hard to see. My vision
is simple and pinholed. I am adrift,
constantly moving, considered
and slow as I majestic my way
through the world. I resist pressure
and avoid implosion. I can survive
when dredged from the deep.

Matthew Rohrer

Poem for Miroslav Holub

The Gloomy Octopus lives
inside the book forever

while the tea kettle is boiling
I can look into its eyes

and it stares back at me
but does not love me

for it is gloomy, and
the octopus inside the book forever

is made of ink that reflects
light and is reflected in the mind

and what the mind makes
says Holub, is only there to shore up emptiness

"the primary and secondary emptiness"
which he never explains

Kathryn Sadakierski

The Octopus Rewritten

The octopus leaves its signature,
Tentacles curling through the water,
Ink written in the currents,
Invisible messages.

Always rewriting itself,
Taking on new shapes,
Agile acrobatics, fluid as paint,
Every letter of the alphabet,

The octopus, elusive, enigmatic,
Slips in and out
Of view,
An inken signature left behind.

People imagine you, the octopus,
As a terrible beauty,
Spidery and serpentine,
Tentacles like long waves

Of Medusa's hair,
Irascible, wrathful, an icy gaze
Turning courage to stone
That crumbles in your presence,

Down in the depths of the ocean,
You are swift and sure;
But do they understand
What it is you say,

Your ink scrawlings,
Smoke signals,
Communicating to the world
A beauty all your own?

You leave your signature,
Ink curled in typewriter ribbons,
As only you, the octopus, could,
Reimagined, not confined
To the murky depths of mystery,
Those shadowy channels of the sea.

Lawrence Schimel

Childhood Aquarium

She did not want me
to kill, dropped goldfish
into brine herself. They
began to die long
before the inky

cloud, the tentacles.
My mother always
averted her eyes.
The lid dropped. Glass shards
flashed like scales, and I

hunted for the thin eel
I'd caught at the beach,
always white with fear
of being noticed:
the white of coral,

the white enamel
of my dresser. It
couldn't disappear
until the lid fell.
Glass broke. The water

broke. The octopus,
like a stomach turned
inside out, still flailed
on the floor between
my mother's legs. Her

hands cupped empty air
above the broken
bowl as if she were
dispensing alms, or
begging for them back.

Tina Schumann

Self-Portrait as Unreliable Narrator

Covert operator,
identity agent—habitual
vertical pronoun

whistling
in the dark. As *in*
as an inside job can be.

Meanwhile from a couch in California...
my brother is choosing oblivion
too soon for the rest of us.

His long foot in permanent rictus
points south. His morphined speech
slurs over the airwaves.

While in the Pacific...sleeping octopus
change colors when dreaming.
Though no one knows what they dream.

Still, I remain content
with the family baggage
and our boneyard heresies.

Bumbling through the usual
bleak parables, I play both
understudy and stagehand.

While the city of Buenos Aires
has built a public park
along their old ramparts,

lovers stroll by
rusted cannons
that point to the sky.

I remain one
with homemade double-blind
tests; placebos at the ready.

Can you see
the human
in my being?

It's debilitating beauty—
fraudulent, carbon based
crackle and bloom.

The last thing
my brother ever said—
OK, I'm ready.

Brenda Shaughnessy

Bakamonotako

Bakamonotako translates roughly into "The Stupid Little Octopus Girl." She's a character in an old Japanese folk tale. I read her story on a plaque outside the Little Sea Monster Museum Sculpture Garden. I thought she was a lot like me.

From a good family of upstanding octopuses, Bakamonotako felt she didn't need all eight of her appendages. Four would do. Two to wash and work and two to walk and wander. To the embarrassment and horror of her family, she let her other four limbs fall into such disuse that they withered and fell away. So she resembled a human being, with two arms and two legs, except that her mouth and her genitalia were the same orifice.

Like all stupid little girls who believe they can best become themselves by becoming unlike themselves, she eventually came to miss her lost limbs. At times, fully tattooed people feel so about their lost original skin. But B's sense of regret ran deeper.

When she matured and tried to have sexual relations as an adult octopus, the limbs she cast off with her mind wrapped around her and bound her, keeping her from any feeling. The phantom tentacles were strong, adult-sized ghosts and angry about losing their body.

Embittered and maddened, Bakamonotako consulted a wise starfish about her future. The starfish said, "You must find the other half of yourself, of your deepest and most private feeling, and you might have to double yourself to do it."

The starfish asked Bakamonotako for twice her usual fee for this advice and the stupid little octopus girl paid half in sand dollars and half in sand dollars she hoped to collect in the future. With only half her limbs, she would need to spend twice as much time scrambling in the sand, so fleshy and vulnerable on the ocean floor, to find these dollars. She could see already how her existence of constantly halving and doubling was playing itself out. Once she'd started this math, she saw she'd never be whole, clear, even.

She had spent her future already, searching for sand dollars to pay the starfish for advice about her future, which had already been determined by her past.

Ella Shively

Cephalopod Smackdown

> *"Australia: Geologist beaten up by 'angriest octopus' on beach"*
> —*BBC News, April 2, 2021*

I've got three hearts that brim with angst,
eight suckered arms about to waste
that clueless smile right off your face.
I'll say, I'm cephalo-*pissed off*, mate!
I know that I unleash my rage
on blameless schmucks but I can't take
the shredded threads of plastic in my gut
for one more day. I've traded vacant shells
for takeaway cups. This mollusk lusts for blood
because the world is warming up!
I'm gruff, but you'd be just the same,
if your whole body was your brain.
And I am nature's soldier, nameless,
launching misplaced anguish
at distressed vacationers. Patience,
patience, I have none, I'll fight
until my cobalt blood runs wine-dark
in the thunderous waves. I will crush
your atoms with my blazing, amber gaze.
Do not mistake my missing vertebrae
for lack of spine. This kraken
will not crawl complacent,
back below the brine.

Martha Silano

Eight Facts about Octopuses

1. It's *octopuses* or *octopodes*, not *octopi*; it's not Latin but Latinized from the Greek.

oktōpous, ("eight-foot"). *Octopus* wasn't coined until 1758, but they've been around for 300 million years (compared to our 300 thousand).

2. 140 million years ago, Octopuses lost their shells. The evolutionary advantages? Squeezing into tight spaces, like drainpipes when they've been confined to an aquarium tank, decide it's time to head to the sea. If they need protection, they grab two coconut shells, curl up inside, or brandish half of one like a shield. Large pieces of seaweed and collage-like conglomerations of shells, corals, and rocks also make for excellent hideouts.

3. Their arms (not tentacles) contain two-thirds more neurons than their brains, which can fire independently. They think with their arms, at times bypassing the brain entirely. An octopus limb sports 240 suckers, each functioning independently. A large sucker can hold up to 35 pounds. Scientists note their grooves and fine hairs, hoping (but failing) to reproduce their knack for adhering. Their suckers can also taste. If an arm breaks off, a new one grows back.

4. For years thought to be solitary, octopuses have recently been found congregating. In the waters near downtown Sydney, aka Octoplis, hundreds hang out in adjacent dens—sparring, wrestling, and high fiving.

5. Octopods can change color up to 177 times an hour. Because color change occurs through tiny pigment-filled sacs, not

hormones, adjustments in camouflage happen in a literal blink of an eye (200 milliseconds). This is 100s of times faster than a chameleon. They can also alter their texture to match surrounding corals, kelp, or rocks, and grow horns. Surprisingly, octopuses are colorblind, but subcutaneous photoreceptor cells allow them to see with their skin.

6. Cheeky, curious, and affectionate, octopuses appear to possess great awareness, sensitivity, and intelligence. In a 1959 paper, researchers noted that rather than pull a lever to receive sardines, "Albert," a test subject, busied himself trying to break the lever clean off, wrestling with it for hours, while repeatedly spraying a whitecoat he didn't seem to fancy. Octopuses have been captured on film parallel playing with schools of fish, playing catch with a pill bottle, and cuddling up in the arms of a human they trust.

7. With his third limb, aka the sex arm, the male octopus places a pack of sperm into the female's mantle cavity. Octopuses "do it" face-to-face for up to six hours. Until her 200,000-400,000 eggs hatch, the female holds her eggs near her mouth for several months, not a problem because she's stopped eating. After they're born, the female experiences "cellular suicide," dying soon after. The male follows a month later. The babies drift away on clouds of plankton for a few weeks before returning to bottom of the sea.

8. You have to go back 750 million years to find the common ancestor between humans and octopuses, a flatworm that emerged 500 million years before the dinosaurs. It has a simple nervous system and primitive light sensors akin to eyes. Octopuses remained invertebrates, have three hearts, blue blood, and spray dark ink when attacked, dulling an attacker's taste and smell. The group of animals octopuses belong to—the cephalopods—were likely Earth's first intelligent beings. They shouldn't be this smart, but they are.

Martha Silano

There's So Much to Admire

about ammonites, I don't know where to begin.
Like this place called Kremmling, Colorado,
where so many died

it's like a graveyard. It's mostly a theory, but some believe
they were spawning under a full moon
when the sea suddenly warmed,

became acidic, and/or lost all its oxygen, or else they died
because there were no offspring, and ammonites
eat their young.

Or that the sky darkened when an asteroid crashed into Yucatan,
which pretty much halted photosynthesis, so bacteria
dominated the seas, as it had

for millions of years before. This one paleontologist on *YouTube*
said "they retain their whole life history in their shells."
I bet we do the same. I bet some creature,

millennia from now, will run tests on our bones, analyzing
the carbon and oxygen isotopes, calculate the acidity
of our oceans, the amount of carbon

in our atmosphere right before the equivalent
of a great spawning extravaganza—
the tides high, the moon's light

forging a glittery path across the dark waves
of Exxon-Mobile, Conoco, and Standard Oil.
Named by Pliny the Elder after Ammon,

an Egyptian god who sported a ram's horn, early collectors
called them *snake stones*, sold them
for their curative powers.

The Blackfeet, noting their resemblance to buffalo,
used them in ceremonies before hunts.
In Germany, the cure for a dry cow:

put a "curie" in the milking pail, while in Rome tucking one
under one's pillow was said to produce
prophetic dreams. Louis Agassiz,

a pal of Cuvier, lecturing on the coiling and uncoiling
of their shells, compared their twisted forms
to the writhing contortions

of a death struggle. Others referred to them as "bizarre forms"
having the "appearance of abnormality." We now know
they were adapting to their environment,

evolving when random mutations proved beneficial, filing
more and more niches until there were 10,000-plus
species, and 30 body types, including *Parapuzosia*,

six feet in diameter. Some resemble hair pins, pointy tipped
carrots. Many retained a spiraling form. If you visit
Kremmling, the first things you'll come upon

are a Subway and a Kum & Go. We've been around for 300,000 years,
but the ammonites hung on for 350 million. They thrived
in methane seeps, a toxic gas that kills us,

adapted to catastrophe until they no longer could, until a sudden
influx of carbon wiped them out. An influx less sudden
than the one we face.

Pam Yve Simon

Octopuses Are Known Problem Solvers

If octopuses dream, then it is
probably brief.
As if a fleeting dream were anything less
than transformational.

You visited me in a dream
to brush my hair.
That was enough.

I woke up, looking for you.
My hair doesn't know
to stop
expecting your tenderness.

Kathryn Smith

Ode to Super Friends and Nature Television

Days when the planet seems particularly poised
for disaster, I wear both my cephalopod T-shirt
and my cephalopod ring. Have you heard of a more

Anthropocene coping mechanism? I do it
for the birds with nowhere to land at the critical
point in their migration, for the skewed seasons,

and the jungle ants with parasite-skewered brains.
Cave dwellers evolve to survive their sealed-over eyes.
Who needs eyes on a planet wobbling its axis

like a Tilt-A-Whirl? No wonder I wake
motion sick, the fact of death and the ocean and
the mouthparts of insects brimming the list of things

I can't control. Wonder Twin powers, activate!
Form of a fang, a blood-thirsty proboscis,
a tidal turnaround. I wear pants the color of a sea

cucumber, wash my octopus shirt on the saltwater setting.
Anything to understand the universe's categories.
Bats aren't birds, but they're winged. Still life and stillbirth

sound like they'd mean the same thing, but they don't.
Mammals are peculiar, our young feeding on us. Humans
are more peculiar yet, building intricate reefs of plastic

and dread. The beauty of birds isn't flight. It's how they let
their young cram pointy beaks down their throats.
On a planet poised for disaster, I track my desires

in a bullet journal, cover my mammary glands
with a boneless bioluminescence. Delicate dangers
of life in the wild dominate my queue. I watch a robin

side-eye me with its bird face, asking what I did
with its family. I've never been good at discerning
the joyful cries of children at play from the backyard

yowl of a cat fight. If I weren't such a creature of habit,
I'd be a creature of soil, tunneling a nest that writhes
the earth's surface. I am sixty percent water and less than one

percent salt, and when ocean levels rise enough to wash us
from our perches, I'll have zero control over my need
to breathe air, which is not in my control to begin with.

Sheila Sondik

Fellow Travelers

a tanka sequence

the captive octopus
matches shapes
for a tasty reward—
we struggle to match fish
to the aquarium's wall labels

frozen squid
and tardigrades
rocketing away
to the space lab—
thaw in good health!

octopuses change colors
in active sleep states—
in REM sleep
I dream of shape-shifting
and eight-armed embraces

William Stafford

Aquarium at Seaside

Groping stars called up from a field,
in silence curled these languid creatures,
abrupt as truth's edge, wander their schedule.
What great rope current braided us apart?
Into that night we follow those lives,
lonely like ours. With my tongue
I touch the glass: millions of years.
It divides the world.

Cecilia Stancell

Goddess

The goddess is rising from the dark
and deep, rising on a matted bed of kelp
from a green storm of waves
because it is time.

She is rising from the salt
of the earth dissolved in earth's first
tears shed in the joy of creation,
in the pain of rending mountains.

She turns to the moon with wide,
bright irises and feels it,
and rises and falls.
The life within and around her is
reaching and sensing with
long and living fingers, like the
alien intelligence of the cephalopod,
brain dispersed through limbs
that live nearly-separate lives,
but which are bound up into one
malleable, wise, and secretive body.

She comes in stealth to the shallows
to see something new,
to show her awe-full face,
to breathe the air for the very first time.

Jennifer K. Sweeney

Octopus Tango

He caresses the outskirts of the dark
reef floor, this *El Mocho* of the sea,
searching for the partner with the most
floreadora to dance the seductive *cortez.*
By the tangled coral, she waits,
tentative, shawls of flesh gracing
her repose.

       Don't try to take big strides. The charm
       of the Argentine tango lies in its apparent simplicity.

He glides deliberate and slow.
She is one of the many
he will promenade with tonight
but for now she is
the only.

       It should be practiced frequently
       so as to make it smooth.

A brazen challenger strikes the scene
and the two *baileadors* tumble in a snakelike
mass of adrenaline until the most agile
tentacle wins. *El Mocho* approaches
a second time, flushed with struggle
and allure. Here the pair is most seductive
as they tread toward an elegant embrace.

       The man must learn to lead with his whole body.

From his bundle of extremities he offers
a sleek tube to her underflesh and begins

the ascent with candor.
She slinks at his side, subtle, demure.
An understated tempo.
They do not attempt the scissors step—
even *Los Silva* would not have been skillful
enough to cross and uncross eight pairs
of legs—but their repertoire is sensuous.

As in the tango, the female decides
when she is done following her partner
but tonight she is hasty.

    The body must glide along without any stops.

Turning her head sharply she flounces
off, *El Mocho* still attached,
flailing about the rocky floor as if
on a leash—an exit
that would challenge the most fiery
slap on the cheek.

Arianne True

Encoded Anatomies

I - limbs

this is how it feels to be boneless
to slide over ground, only muscle

but when I lie down, bone-heavy,
each line draws a human body on the bed

how wild to still feel tired after days of rest,
how wild to still/have a racing brain

watching it walk, each step a lash
a soft curl unfurls along long limbs

that is not how I move anymore
not today, at least, not now

something is in my heart, or my nerves
something slows and numbs, I tremble

doctors will come with offerings
I already hold open and still

whole creatures live this slowly
cycles of torpor, breath, collapse

II - mantle, with contents

I used to think diagnosis inevitable,
to think all wrong things detectable
and known. Certainty has passed

through my organs transformed.
Something as soft and malleable
as an octopus has a hard, sharp

beak somewhere in the supple.
You can't see it from here. But
there it is, and venom (call it

poison) spreads the same whether
or not you watch. Know what bit.
I'll see a heart specialist next week.

I wonder if she knows which
tender set of cells grows itself
three hearts: one for each set

of gills, and one for the rest
of everything. There are not
second and third hearts

powering my lungs. She knows
that already, before meeting.
What will she and my body

say to each other in that office?
I've become more afraid, leave
trails of ink wherever I go.

III - (it's not all in your) head (but it's there too)

You look last at my eyes. We meet them so rarely these days.
You know what it is to be sick like this, a body full of
thresholds and tipping points. Too many people
I love are sick. From when we didn't die. A
radula is a rasp, is a ribbon. In octopuses,
balance is fluid floating in fluid. This is
older than two summers. Roots in
the brain, the nervous system.
Your life hides in your soft
shell. Ripples (quiet). No
one knows what's
wrong. What
happened.
But you
do.

Emily Tuszynska

Bobtail Squid by Starlight (*Euprymna scolopes*)

Just two thumbs long, the creature of a single season,
she's round and squat as a dumpling.
Her chromatophores flicker and settle in speckles
across her translucence. She wants nothing
more than to hide. She's seafloor and rock;
she's two mirrored eyes that see
without being seen.
      Startled, she scuds backward.
In the place where she was, an inked duplicate
dissolves into nothing. She's elsewhere,
backing into a pocket of agitated sand,
patting crystalline grains over her protuberant mantle.

She sees in two directions: one eye for what hunts her,
one for what she hunts. In darkness she shimmers
with symbiont light: *Vibrio* luminosity
in her mantle's crypts, phosphorescence
sheltered, reflected, shuttered, and lensed
to hide her silhouette against tropical starlight.

Unstealthy human, splashing through seafoam,
haven't you also wished yourself invisible?
Aren't you tired of your obstinate self?
Euprymna bobs in the shallows.
The moon rises and she matches its downwelling light
until even her shadow is lost in the glow.
From dark tides she slips into starshine and moonlight.

Barbara Ungar

Dumbo Octopus

(*Grimpotheutis*)

Dumbos are bellshaped, semi-
translucent, with huge eyes
and fins like elephant ears
they flap to move
with peculiar grace,

or hover above the deep
sea floor, resembling
small umbrellas. Startled,
they invert like
umbrellas blown inside out.

Also called winged octopus
or jellyheads, Dumbos
live in the abyssal depths.
The deep so vast
and Dumbos so rare, she's

always ready, with eggs at
various stages. If
she gets lucky, he gives her
a sperm packet
to stash until she's safe.

Newborn, octopuses can
fend off killer whales and
sharks. Intelligent, they sleep
like us, dream and
learn. Dumbos see only

bioluminescence. When
our latest craft descend
to their depths, can they even
perceive us? They're
not threatened by us. Yet.

O

Cody Walker

From Sonnet to Stage

In liquid murk, the squid doth lurk.
He wrangles rhymes. (Don't laugh; it's work.)
What chimes with tuna? Big kahuna.
Who charms a clam? Martha Graham.

The squid's poems scan! They bump and spin!
(Their meanings are a little thin.)
Prosodically, the squid's effusive!
(His aims remain a bit elusive.)

He contradicts himself like Whitman;
But labels, ehh, they don't fit, man.
He's of two minds; he has three hearts;
He moves in modest fits and starts;

This totem beast of verse, reversal,
Is ready for his dress rehearsal.

Cody Walker

You're Telling That Story Again

About the googly-eyed glass squid, how it beats anything, a free
motor scooter, a trip to two weeks ago, a slice of blueberry pie—
and the whole time you're talking I'm thinking about this tree I
saw earlier, this Tree of Life–type tree with a spiked haircut that
forced its shadow across the rock face and into the sound, how
the whole island appeared suddenly in relation to that shadow,
and the only reason I'm telling you any of this, the only reason
I'm trying to interrupt your story, the memory of your having
told your story, is because I'm kind of in love with you, but if
I told you properly, my voice would turn see-through, and if I
wrote it down properly, my ink would run into the water.

JR Walsh

Reef Population

The dugongs are crying when they should be grazing. Vegetarian dishes are harder to find. Morale is destroyed as per The Order of the *Asteroidea*. Bleaching is trending. The sea stars are regenerative carnivores and venture capitalists. It's their fault the urchins are urchins and urchins never learn nothing. But the last straw? The leaked photographs; maybe the algae strike. This reef's been burned enough. The idealism of common sea stars!

*

Cranky algae presses a strike without union backing. There's planning in the desert. Old managers are deposed. It's hush baby then, when woolly lawsuits are sewn up like dead scrolls. Anthropology throws the book at the sea stars, ignoring no-contest pleas and oceanic bends of knee. Calls them starfish, risking disbarment. Nobody tells the dugongs. They'll go to tears or start drinking.

**

Marry in coral, bury in coral. Revenge isn't a dish at all, it's a plastic baggie seeping plastic. Urchins watch and watch. The dugongs pray for time-elapse photography to breathe quicker, vegetate with purpose. Breathe streaky and exhale where you stand. Sea stars are born again to climb.

***

Molluscan feet found in mouths so far below, beaky as a chatty raptors. Big beautiful brains bring their own tanks. So much cartilage, it's sacrilege. Octopus can't hear that polluting schooner so good, but, the lowest of frequencies offends, upends frequently. Who you calling sucker, or was it saccular? One too many whale concerts certainly hasn't helped, even though they brought the whole light show. The dugongs are silent among cuttlefish. In the seagrass, both eat and cry, but only cuttlefish make love under the stars.

Lylium Walsh

O. **regulare**

Before the modern nautilus—
Before squid, octopi, or cuttlefish—
Floated ancient *Orthoceras*.

Long, straight horn. Not much muscle. Ocean floor.
Mysterious and primeval.

Alive in Middle Ordovician:
Alive when the land first bore spores,
When little meteors fell
Between two intense extinction events.

Forbearer of cephalopods
During rapid diversification
As radiation fell from sky
Or other unknown causes made life spread.

Bones born of compressed time scattered
In lime from Sweden to the Baltic States.
A Triassic ghost lineage
Frequently mistaken for *Baculites.*
Both now paperweights for purchase.

Michael Waters

Diogenes

The water lay flat to the horizon and so clear
You could swim far out past the coral reef
And, looking down, still see the sandy shelf
Tilting below pale, coffin-shaped feet.
Barracuda hung like mobiles in the blue layers,
Cool gunmetal, unwavering, purposeful.
The days were long, and I wanted nothing,
Though sometimes I thought I wanted truth
Until the burning, colorless liqueurs confused me.
I was grateful for their little brushfires in my body.
The days were long, yes, and growing longer.
I strolled through the evening throngs,
The tourists in loud shirts and straw hats,
And dined alone among them while ancient,
Indigenous men bearing guitars and whittled flutes
Shuffled table to table, birthing once more
That one, lilting, Incan melody everyone hums.
In the morning, when clumps of flies
Blackened honeyed scrolls tacked to rafters,
When truth prodded me again
With its trumpet blare of heat and light,
I snorkeled toward families of green squid,
Alert, throbbing, horizontal, lit-from-within
Coke bottles teasing me forth

As if I could unloosen my skin
Like a shirt forgotten on the beach
To be borne away at night by lapping waters,
As if I might join those inky creatures
To spend my days reaching always for the nothing
That remains just beyond my grasp.

Beth Wilks

Giant Pacific Octopus (*Enteroctopus dofleini*)

Cassondra Windwalker

mother octopus

does her hunger drift away from her,
I wonder, like krill on the current,
or do her insides ache every day
as she stands watch
over her innumerable brood,
is each lost meal an act of will,
a choice of their future over her present?

perhaps in time she forgets
that she ever ate,
remembers not the splitting and tearing
but only the plunging and the soaring,
the sinking and the spinning and the inking,
the sensation of the ocean's thousand fingers
on her flesh: does an octopus feel
each color that flashes over her skin
as its own thrill, does each hue
carry a different, specific memory
that she clings now she has been relegated
to darkness in this den, to just one color,
the color of silence and subterfuge
that must last till her clutch emerges?

she was taught nothing
she will teach nothing
but still she has learned so much

and it will all end here,
in a bubbling, flurrying fury of baby octopuses
scattering in the salty water,
each so entirely alone,
alone as she is, sinking empty to the ocean floor.

Catherine Wing

Self-portrait with Eight Brains at the End of Eight Limbs

Don't speak of my face—what matters
is my hands and how they make
a sucker twitch. My body is an arc
that rides a moment full circle

into its occasion. I guess you'd say
I'm an alternative sort of organization
ink along the thought line, unfurling
into sense. I don't come directly

and never call me like a dog.
Over-extended by definition, a digging cogitation
in my garden of scalloped coral shells.
I possess a singular and self-winding

clockwork and can unspool the thread
of any given carpet to catch its pattern.
In short, there is no problem
I can't squeeze my puzzle through.

Deborah Woodard

Sailor & Cephalopod Quartet

1. **Under the Tutelage of a Beak**

Reef squid quickly become weathered, dying young like sailors
in pigtails, with grave soft mouth folds. Seamen's obituaries
are sealed, then sprinkled with salt water. Translucent, the bluish
envelopes resemble squid flotillas dropping before striking.
Now, insignias try to break loose under the tutelage of a beak,
similar in shape to a parrot's. And nearby, a sailor begins
recording color changes on underwater tablets. He'd been
on board long enough, had eaten afternoon sunlight.
(He was grave and from Vladivostok.) Squid signal alarm:
their brow ridges turning bright gold while their central arms
whiten. But the envelopes stay blue. One squid tops another
squid and fights. It's like the way a coin expresses itself
by flipping. Color patterns flash, while the younger of the two
puffs up in the face of this threat. They both pull things
from chromophores like emptying envelopes.

2. **And the Sailors Stayed Bunched**

The envelope teased the eye, inviting intense watching.
Two little squid arose, showing off black naval jackets.
Gold trim celebrated the largest eye to body ratio in the
annals of deep-sea fishing. An obit sped to Vladivostok,
with its inner pedaling. And the sailors stayed bunched,
heads lowered, moving toward the back of the deck.
When approached by a predator, they curled up as one.
In autumn, blood throbs against the sailors' pigtails.
Absence pelts down, melding our twin squid briefly
before they die. Compared to most on the deck, squids'
eyes loved staying sealed shut.

3. **Spilt Ink is All Too Common**

The letter I received was on pale paper, slashed
by a cuttlebone. To signal others, squid excrete a reddish
dye to match the stamps. Meanwhile, the pigtail falls ill,
despite Vladie's attempts to secure it. Pigtail throws fits
till Old Ocean unbraids and washes it. A naval jacket
exhibits brocade's heavy jaws. Blotches form on insignias,
though the collar stays pressed. Grounded, the hull
is a compulsive predator, with separate holds for parcels.
Sailors kneel beside it to check for squid. Spilt ink is all
too common. The reef often turns maroon for potential
predators, wrapping them in bare branches. This made me
think of Vladie. He tends to blush if the squid approach.

4. **Washed Out with Baby Shampoo**

To prevent fogging in the mask, Vladie washed it out with
baby shampoo. The female squid placed the male squid's
packet in her seminal receptacle. Granted, the pair was then
essentially washed up. In point of fact, they'd courted for
almost an hour, and she'd already been stroked by his tentacles.
He'd blown water at her to calm her, then jetted gently away.
Dying, she was startled by our sailor, from whom light pulsed
like signals from a male squid. The blotch of his wet suit
intercepted her leaving, delayed evolution's miscreant whim.
In the soft folds of his thumb, he wore a gold ring he often
twisted, even underwater. Ashore and recapping the shampoo,
Vladie felt buoyed up by a modicum of order. His ring shone
like a coin or a teardrop. Swimming over dark sand,
the female squid laid her eggs in pigtail clusters.

Susan J. Wurtzburg

Space Squids

Hawaiian Bobtail Squids, trip of a lifetime,
resident cephalopods, international space station.
Bulbous heads with peach-mottled skin soar
among the stars, tentacles float in zero gravity.

Astronauts tend their needs, smile at these oddities,
perform tests requested by earth-bound scientists.
Space squids' kin flash through ocean depths
while these ones fly above, five miles per second.

Jeffrey Yang

Octopus

Tikopians believe the octopus
is both a mountain with tentacle-
streams, and the sun
with its rays, so should not be eaten.
The mystery of metaphor is
nearly lost to us, as if
only the illusion of metaphor
remains. Or the myth of metaphor.
Or metaphor without ikon.
Rousseau writes:
The first speech was all in poetry.
Or poetry's reasoning
was the first figure
of speech. Palin-
genesis of word (*butter
bird*) mind's
forms, reveals
mind ether, spirit
unhindered.

Jeffrey Yang

Squid

In the U.S. Nemo's *Nautilus*
was attacked by a giant cuttle-
fish squid—*What a freak of nature!*
a bird's beak on a mollusc!—
But a friend tells me that
in Mexico it was a giant octopus.
How profound translation
shapes our dreams! And dream
a silent translation of a dream
the way squids chromatophorically
communicate. And translation
a dream of One. *Translate,*
follow up on, follow after...

Matthew Zapruder

Glass Octopus

The mesopelagic touched the underside
of a boat my father could only dream
of building. When he died, I turned
his fortune into a sturdy vessel that churned
through countless waves, searching
for a place where everything is equidistant.
I stayed for years, going again and again
down in the chamber of a lowered bell.
Through thick glass I saw wondrous
things words cannot capture, creatures
that glowed and ones that did not, great
shapes looming up then falling back
into deeper regions, plants whose gestures
suggested sentience. This became
my life. Finally I saw her, the rarely
observed close relative of the telescope.
She looked like an x-ray of a lightbulb
transparently ate an orange crayon
attached to a tangle of those small
white xmas lights that used to run across
the ceilings of those rooms we lived in
for many years during the quiet age. She
came to touch my window, as if to silently
let me know she was not asking
for something I have never been able to give.
Through her I could see the deep
layer where she lives. Until that moment
I didn't realize I feared I was the predator
hunting for what was never there.
But here she was, deep where no light
passes through her radula. Moving
from one lightless spot to another

she leaves no glowing trace. She needs
no mate. I watched her as I rose back up
into the blue light that already knew
what I had finally discovered. To be
truly sad you have to go elsewhere.

Mari Zeng

Peptides

In shallow sunlight, I wake up to the tickle of peptide
tomorrows;
today is the last day as an unmated female.
Blood chooses my Time. I choose my crevice.

Will you grant me this burden?
Canvas, pigment, muse,
Dissolved, mother and host.

Eight-armed words have no edges.
Copper, chromatophore, hectocotylus,
Beak. Alright, one edge.

Do or die or do and die.
Doomed semelparous meeting of hearts hearts hearts hearts
    hearts hearts.

My hundred-thousand children will inherit the earth.

CONTRIBUTORS

Claire Hsu Accomando was born in Switzerland to Chinese and French-Armenian parents. Her poems have appeared in *Atlanta Review, Mudfish, California Quarterly,* and elsewhere. Her memoir, *Love and Rutabaga: A Remembrance of the War Years* (St. Martin's Press), was translated into French and published in 2020 (L'Harmattan).

Sally Albiso has published three chapbooks and two full-length collections. Honors include *The Comstock Review's* Muriel Craft Bailey Memorial Award, the Robert Frost Foundation Poetry Award, the Camber Press Poetry Chapbook Award, and three nominations for the Pushcart Prize. Sally passed away in October 2019.

Amy Ash is the author of *The Open Mouth of the Vase* and co-editor of *Imaginative Teaching through Creative Writing: A User's Guide for Secondary Classrooms.* She is Associate Professor of English and Director of Creative Writing at Indiana State University.

M. C. Aster was born in Yugoslavia and has lived on three continents. Drawing inspiration from human history, nature, and mythology, Aster's poems and writing have appeared in many journals and publications including *Painted Bride Quarterly.* Aster lives in Southern California and fosters two endangered Mojave Desert tortoises.

Hadara Bar-Nadav is an NEA fellow and author of several award-winning books of poetry, among them *The Animal Is Chemical* (forthcoming), *The New Nudity, Lullaby* (with Exit Sign), *The Frame Called Ruin,* and *A Glass of Milk to Kiss Goodnight,* as well as the chapbooks *Fountain and Furnace* and *Show Me Yours.* She is also co-author with Michelle Boisseau of the best-selling textbook *Writing Poems, 8th ed.* Hadara is a Professor of English and teaches in the MFA program at the University of Missouri-Kansas City.

Cathy Barber's poetry has been published in the journals *Slant, SLAB, Tule Review, Kestrel*, the anthologies *Rewilding: Poems for the Environment* and *Fire and Rain: Ecopoetry of California*, and has been nominated for a Best of the Net. She has an abecedarian chapbook *Aardvarks, Bloodhounds, Catfish, Dingoes* (Dancing Girl Press, 2018) and *Once: A Golden Shovel Collection* from Kelsay Books. She is a graduate of the Vermont College of Fine Arts MFA program and makes her home in Cleveland Heights, Ohio. www.cathybarber.com

Nicky Beer is a bi/queer writer, and the author of *Real Phonies and Genuine Fakes* (Milkweed, 2022), winner of the 2023 Lambda Literary Award for Bisexual Poetry. She's received honors from the Guggenheim Foundation, the NEA, the Poetry Foundation, and more. She teaches at the University of Colorado Denver.

"Ad Hominem" and "Frost on the Octopus" were originally published in *The Octopus Game* (Carnegie Mellon Univ. Press).

Ahimsa Timoteo Bodhrán is author of Archipiélagos, *Antes y después del Bronx: Lenapehoking,* and *South Bronx Breathing Lessons,* editor of the international queer Indigenous issue of *Yellow Medicine Review,* and co-editor of the Native dance/movement/performance issue of *Movement Research Performance Journal.*

"Entreaty: invite from the ocean floor" originally appeared in *Vallum.*

Karina Borowicz is the author of *Rosetta* (Ex Ophidia, 2021), *Proof* (Codhill Press, 2014), and *The Bees Are Waiting* (Marick Press, 2011). A French bilingual volume of new and selected works, *Tomates de septembre,* was published by Cheyne-éditeur in 2020. Visit her website at karinaborowicz.com.

"Fist" originally appeared in *qarrtsiluni.*

Janet Bowdan's poems have appeared in *APR, Tahoma Literary Review, The Rewilding Anthology, Sequestrum,* and elsewhere. The editor of Common Ground Review, she teaches at Western New England University and lives in Northampton, Massachusetts, with her husband, their son, a vocal cat, and a book-nibbling chinchilla.

Elizabeth Bradfield is the author of five poetry collections, most recently *Toward Antarctica,* and co-editor of the anthologies *Cascadia Field Guide: Art, Ecology, Poetry* and *Broadsided Press: Fifteen Years of Poetic/Artistic Collaboration.* Editor-in-chief of Broadsided, Liz lives on Cape Cod, works as a naturalist, and teaches at Brandeis University. www.ebradfield.com

"Sweater for a Giant Squid" appeared in *Interpretive Work* (Arktoi Books/Red Hen Press, 2008).

Poet and photographer **Ronda Piszk Broatch** lives in Kingston, WA, situated on northwest coast Suquamish and Port Gamble S'Klallam tribal land.

"It was the year of considering time travel" originally appeared in *Chaos Theory for Beginners* (MoonPath Press, 2023).

Rebecca Brock's work appears in *The Threepenny Review, CALYX, Whale Road Review,* and elsewhere. In 2022, she won the Kelsay Women's Poetry Contest and *The Comstock Review's* Muriel Craft Bailey Award. Her books include *Each Bearing Out* and *The Way Land Breaks.* Find more of her work at www.rebeccabrock.org.

"Octopus" was a finalist in the 2021 Joy Harjo Poetry Prize at *Cutthroat, A Journal for the Arts.*

"Octopus" first appeared in *The Way Land Breaks* by Sheila-Na-Gig Editions.

Meg Caldwell is a queer poet and essayist from the Midwest. She currently resides in Florida where she is an accessible education teacher and Neurodivergent Student Advocate. You can find her on Instagram @MegCaldwellCorson and IRL fishing off bridges, reading comics, or trying to identify trees in her neighborhood.

Nancy Canyon is published in *Nature's Healing Spirit*, Raven Chronicles' *Take a Stand: Art Against Hate, True Stories II & III, Last Call, Ice Cream Poems, Water~Stone Review, Fourth Genre, Floating Bridge Review,* and more. She holds an MFA in Creative Writing from PLU, works as a writing coach for The Narrative Project, and paints in her Historic Fairhaven Art studio. *Celia's Heaven* (novel) and *Saltwater* (poetry) are available at villagebooks.com. See more at www.nancycanyon.com.

Alaskan Poet, Moon Gazer, Raven Watcher, Way-finder, Northern Trekker, Teacher. **Kersten Christianson** derives inspiration from wild places, wandering ambles, and road trips without any real destination. Kersten serves as poetry editor of the quarterly journal *Alaska Women Speak.* Her latest collection of poetry is *Curating the House of Nostalgia* (Sheila-Na-Gig Editions, 2020).

Joanne M. Clarkson's sixth poetry collection *Hospice House* was released by MoonPath Press in 2023. Her poems have been published in such journals as *Poetry Northwest, Nimrod, Western Humanities Review,* and *Beloit Poetry Journal.* Clarkson lives in Port Townsend, WA, by the sea.

Will Cordeiro has work published in *AGNI, Bennington Review,* and *The Threepenny Review.* Will won the Able Muse Book Award for *Trap Street.* Will is also co-author of *Experimental Writing: A Writers' Guide and Anthology,* forthcoming from Bloomsbury. Will co-edits Eggtooth Editions and lives in Guadalajara, Mexico.

Brittney Corrigan's poetry collections include *Solastalgia, Daughters, Breaking, Navigation,* and *40 Weeks.* She was raised in Colorado and lives in Portland, Oregon, where she is an alumna and employee of Reed College. She is currently at work on her first short story collection. For more information, visit brittneycorrigan.com.

Kevin Craft lives in Seattle and directs the Written Arts Program at Everett Community College. For 20 years he served as a faculty director of the University of Washington's Writers in Rome program. His books include *Solar Prominence, Vagrants & Accidentals,* and *Traverse* (Lynx House Press, 2023). Editor of *Poetry Northwest* from 2009–2016, he now serves Executive Editor of Poetry NW Editions.

"Linear B" was first published in *Vagrants & Accidentals* (UW Press 2017).

Stephanie Crofts (opening quote) is an assistant professor at the College of the Holy Cross, Worcester MA. She studies biomechanics and functional morphology, using principles from physics and engineering to understand how organisms function in a physical word. Put another way: she pokes organisms to see what happens. Sometimes they poke back.

John Davis is a polio survivor and the author of *Gigs and The Reservist.* His work has appeared recently in *DMQ Review, Iron Horse Literary Review,* and *Terrain.org.* He lives on an island in the Salish Sea.

Claire Dawson lives in Minnesota where she writes about nature and family and delightful things like cephalopods. She won the 2021 Saint Paul Almanac Caroll Connelly Initiative for Poets and Writers Contest and is currently at work on a novel.

Lynn Domina is the author of several books, including *Corporal Works, Framed in Silence,* and *Inland Sea.* She teaches English at Northern Michigan University and serves as Creative Writing Editor of *The Other Journal.* She lives with her family in Marquette, Michigan.

Timothy Donnelly's books include *Chariot* (Wave Books, 2023), *The Problem of the Many* (Wave Books, 2019), and *The Cloud Corporation* (Wave Books, 2011). Winner of the Poetry Society of America's Alice Fay di Castagnola Award and The Paris Review's Bernard F. Connors Prize, Donnelly teaches at Columbia University.

"Panspermia" is the name given to the theory that life is seeded throughout the universe via meteors and such, and recently it has been surmised that that's how our beloved octopi came to occupy Earth's waters.

Merridawn Duckler is a writer from Oregon, author of *Interstate* (dancing girl press) and *Idiom* (Washburn Prize, Harbor Review.) New work in *Seneca Review, Women's Review of Books, Interim, Posit.* Fellowships/awards include Yaddo, Southampton Poetry Conference, Poets on the Coast. She's an editor at *Narrative* and at the philosophy journal *Evental Aesthetics.*

Liza Katz Duncan is the author of *Given* (Autumn House Press, 2023), Autumn House Press Rising Writer Prize winner. Her poems have appeared or are forthcoming in *About Place Journal,* Academy of American Poets *Poem-a-Day, AGNI, The Kenyon Review, Poetry Northwest,* and elsewhere. She received support for her work from the Bread Loaf Environmental Writers' Conference,

Poets & Writers, and the Tucson Festival of Books. She teaches English as a Second Language in New Jersey public schools.

Camille T. Dungy is the author of the book-length narrative *Soil: The Story of a Black Mother's Garden.* She has also written four collections of poetry, including *Trophic Cascade.* She edited *Black Nature: Four Centuries of African American Nature.* A University Distinguished Professor at Colorado State University, Dungy's honors include the 2021 Academy of American Poets Fellowship, a 2019 Guggenheim Fellowship, an American Book Award, and fellowships from the NEA in both prose and poetry.

"Characteristics of Life" first appeared in *Trophic Cascade* (Wesleyan University Press).

Leanne Dunic is a multidisciplinary artist. Her book of lyric prose and photographs, *Wet,* is forthcoming with Talonbooks in Spring 2024. Leanne lives on the unceded and occupied Traditional Territories of the Musqueam, Squamish, and Tsleil-Waututh First Nations.

Natalie Dupille is a cartoonist and illustrator based in Seattle, WA. Dupille is a contributor to a number of local and national publications including *The New Yorker, Playboy, The L.A. Times,* and *The Stranger.* Dupille's work has also been supported by the Henry Art Gallery, Short Run Seattle, Atlantic Center for the Arts, Centrum, and Yiddishkayt. Most recently, she has been exploring neon watercolors and risograph printing.

Northwest Homegrown appeared in *The Seattle Weekly,* Vol 41, Iss 11, Nov 2016.

Amy Eisner teaches creative writing at the Maryland Institute College of Art (MICA), helping undergraduates develop as poets and MFA students integrate writing into their art practices.

Her poems have appeared in journals including *Fence, The Journal, Nimrod, Reed, Sugar House Review,* and *Washington Square,* as well as a few galleries. She enjoys poetry games and cross-disciplinary collaboration.

Katy E. Ellis is the author of the novel-length prose poem *Home Water, Home Land* (Tolsun Books) and three chapbooks, including *Night Watch,* winner of the 2017 Floating Bridge Press chapbook competition. Her work has appeared in many literary journals in the US and Canada and she has twice been nominated for a Pushcart Prize.

Heather Eudy holds an MFA in Poetry from San Diego State University, and her first book of poetry, *Bills of Lading,* was published in *Lantern Tree: Four Books of Poems* (City Works Press, 2012), winner of the San Diego Book Award for best poetry anthology.

Lynn Finger's poems appear in *8Poems, Drunk Monkeys,* and *ONE ART: a journal of poetry.* Lynn's poetry chapbook, *The Truth of Blue Horses* was published by Alien Buddha Press. She was nominated for 2021 and 2022 Best of the Net Anthology. Lynn edits *Harpy Hybrid Review.* Her Twitter is @sweetfirefly2.

Mark A. Fisher is a writer, poet, and playwright living in Tehachapi, CA. His poetry has appeared in: *Reliquiae, Silver Blade, Young Ravens Literary Review,* and many other places. His poem "there are fossils" (originally published in *Silver Blade*) came in second in the 2020 Dwarf Stars Speculative Poetry Competition.

Amber Flame is an interdisciplinary artist, writer, activist and educator, garnering residencies with Hedgebrook, Baldwin for the Arts, and more. Flame's first collection, *Ordinary Cruelty,* published in 2017 through Write Bloody Press. Flame's second book, *apocrifa,* a love story told in verse, launched 2023 from

Red Hen Press. She is at work on a film and an album. Flame is a queer Black dandy mama who falls hard for a jumpsuit and some fresh kicks.

"an octopus escapes the fishing net: *advice for my daughter as cephalopod*" was originally published in *Ordinary Cruelty* (Write Bloody Press, 2017).

Catherine Fletcher is a writer based in Virginia. Recent work has appeared in *The Broadkill Review, The Inflectionist Review, New World Writing, Kissing Dynamite,* and the concert series Concept Lab. She is a Virginia Commission for the Arts Fellow (2022) and a Creature Conserve Mentee (2022-23). She has received fellowships from Arizona State University, Queens Council on the Arts, Brooklyn Arts Council, and others. Learn more at cafletcher.blogspot.com.

"^{20}Ca" was originally published in *The Hopper* (Green Writers Press).

Gabriela Denise Frank is a transdisciplinary storyteller, editor, and educator. Her work appears in *BOMB Magazine, True Story, DIAGRAM, Northwest Review, The Rumpus,* and elsewhere. The author of *Pity She Didn't Stay 'Til the End* (Bottlecap Press), she serves as creative nonfiction editor of *Crab Creek Review.* www.gabrieladenisefrank.com

Octo-Blot first appeared on the cover of *Northwest Review.*

Emily Franklin is the author of more than twenty books. Her work has been published in *The New York Times, The London Sunday Times*, and *Guernica*, as well as featured on National Public Radio, and named notable by the Association of Jewish Libraries. Her debut poetry collection is *Tell Me How You Got Here* (Terrapin Books, 2021). Her novel, *The Lioness of Boston*, about the life of Isabella Stewart Gardner, was published by Godine Books in 2023.

Kelly Froh is a comics artist and co-founder/Executive Director of Short Run Comix & Arts Festival in Seattle. Previous works were published in *Moss, Burning House Press, Poetry Northwest, The Seattle Weekly, The Women's Review of Books,* and *Popula.* Find more of her art at cargocollective.com/kefroh.

Sarah Kilch Gaffney is a writer, brain injury advocate, and homemade caramel aficionado living in Maine. You can find her work at www.sarahkilchgaffney.com.

Heidi Geis is a Seattle-based poet and artist. She doesn't remember exactly when she fell in love with cephalopods but she is very glad she did.

Dean Gessie has won or placed in more than 90 international literary competitions. Dean was included in The 64 Best Poets of 2018 and The 64 Best Poets of 2019 by Black Mountain Press in North Carolina. Additionally, Dean was a medal winner for the Nosside Poetry Prize in Italy. He also won the Enizagam Poetry Contest in California, the Ageless Authors Poetry Contest in Texas, and the Frank O'Hara Poetry Prize in Massachusetts.

Jessica Gigot is a poet, farmer, and writing coach. She lives on a little sheep farm in the Skagit Valley in Washington State. Her second book of poems, *Feeding Hour,* won a Nautilus Award and was a finalist for the 2021 Washington State Book Award. Her writing and reviews appear in publications such as *The New York Times, Seattle Times, Orion, Terrain.org, Ecotone,* and *Poetry Northwest.* Her memoir *A Little Bit of Land* was published by OSU Press in 2022.

Gabby Gilliam lives in the DC metro area with her husband and son. Her poetry has most recently appeared in *One Art, Plant-Human Quarterly, The Ekphrastic Review, Pure Slush, Deep Overstock, Vermillion, MacQueen's Quinterly,* and *Equinox.* You can find her

online at gabbygilliam.squarespace.com or on Facebook at
www.facebook.com/GabbyGilliamAuthor.

Terry Godbey's poetry collections are *Hold Still*, a finalist for
the Main Street Rag Poetry Book Award; *Beauty Lessons*, winner
of the *Quercus Review* Poetry Book Award; *Behind Every Door*,
winner of the *Slipstream* Poetry Chapbook Contest; and *Flame*.
Her poems have also appeared in *Rattle*, *Poet Lore*, *Crab Creek
Review*, *Florida Review,* and *Dogwood*. She works as a writer at
Marriott Vacations Worldwide in Orlando, Florida.

Adriana Grant's poetry has appeared in *Caketrain Journal*,
Diagram, and *LIT*. Two books feature her work: *Wanting Is Easier
Than Having* by Debra Baxter (Publication Studio) and *Poetry
on Wheels: An Anthology of King County's Poetry on Buses Program
1997-2005* (Floating Bridge Press). Adriana lives in Dover, New
Hampshire.

Lee Gulyas teaches at Western Washington University. She
received a Washington State Artist Trust Grant and her work
has appeared in journals including *The Common*, *Tinderbox*, *Los
Angeles Review*, *Passages North*, *Aquifer*, *Jet Fuel Review*, *Barrelhouse*,
reDIVIDer, and *Sweet: A Literary Confection*. Her house is on land,
but the sea is her home. You can often find her in tidepools.

Susan E. Hamilton has kept the right side of her brain thriving
with poetry during her careers in oceanography, biochemistry,
and medical writing. Her poems have appeared in Pacific
Northwest publications including *Belletrist*, *Floating Bridge
Review*, *Switched-on Gutenberg*, *Arnazella*, and *West Wind Review*.
Her first chapbook, *Informed Consent*, was published by Finishing
Line Press in 2018.

Jennifer Harrison has published eight poetry collections, most
recently *Anywhy* (Black Pepper 2018). She founded The Dax
Poetry Collection at the University of Melbourne, and co-judges

the annual Ann Morgan Prize for the Australian Association for Infant Mental Health. In 2012 she was awarded the Christopher Brennan Award for sustained contribution to Australian poetry.

"The Giant Australian Cuttlefish" was first published in *Poetry & Ideas: Text and Images*; and was reprinted in the author's collection *Anywhy* (Black Pepper 2018).

Matthea Harvey is the author of five books of poetry and two books for children. She most recently collaborated on a musical oratorio, *The Temp*, with Taylor Ho Bynum, creating the libretto by erasing *The Tempest*.

"My Octopus Orphan" appeared in *If the Tabloids Are True, What Are You?* (Graywolf, 2014).

James Hoch is the author of *Miscreants, A Parade of Hands,* and *The Last Pawnshop in New Jersey.* His poems have appeared in *Best American Poetry, Kenyon Review, Poetry Daily, Tin House,* and many other publications. Originally from New Jersey, he resides in the Hudson Valley and is professor of creative writing at Ramapo College and guest faculty at Sarah Lawrence College.

"Polycardial" was previously published in *Thrush*, Hoch's collection *The Last Pawnshop in New Jersey* (Louisiana State University Press, 2022), and was selected by Major Jackson for *The Slowdown.*

Rebecca Hoogs is the author of *Self-Storage* (Stephen F. Austin University Press) which was a finalist for the 2013 Washington State Book Award in Poetry, and a chapbook, *Grenade* (GreenTower Press). Her poems have appeared in *Poetry, AGNI, FIELD, Crazyhorse,* and others. She is the Executive Director of Seattle Arts & Lectures.

Shurouq Ibrahim is an Arab-American poet residing in
Columbus, Ohio. She holds an MA in 21st Century Literature
from the University of Lincoln, U.K., and is currently a
doctoral student in the Department of Comparative Studies
at The Ohio State University. Her poetry is often inspired by
her life and experiences in the United States, England, and the
West Bank, Palestine. Her work has appeared in *Barzakh Poetry
Journal*, *Prospectus Literary Review*, *Welter Literary Journal*, and
Yale's *Perch Magazine*.

Anissa Lynne Johnson is a writer and speaker from Michigan's
Upper Peninsula. More often than not, you can find her
combing for beach glass or watching movies that *sigh* never
win awards. She's currently working on her debut novel, a
Tom-Hanks-obsessed romantic comedy. Say hello and read
more at anissalynnejohnson.com.

Britta Johnson (front and back endpaper art) is a Seattle-
based artist who makes video installations, short films, and
community projects. For the most part, she makes stop-motion
animated installations that explore natural phenomena, with a
special focus on light, texture, and movement. Her work can be
found on her website, www.thekmpi.net.

Clare Johnson is a dyke-identified writer + artist, with
fellowships from Jack Straw, Hugo House, Mineral School, and
Crosstown Arts, and funding including 4Culture and Allied Arts.
For 15+ years Clare's created a post-it every night to hold onto
something from each ending day, making 5,000+ pieces so far.

"Post-it Note Project" (continuing perpetually 2005–present):
previously published as part of the poem "There's Something
Else" in *Seattle Review of Books*, where excerpts from the project
were published from 2017-2020.

Jen Karetnick is the author of 11 poetry collections, including
Inheritance with a High Error Rate (winner of the 2022 Cider Press
Review Book Award, forthcoming 2024) and the chapbook
What Forges Us Steel: The Judge Judy Poems (Alternating Current
Press, forthcoming 2024). She co-founded *SWWIM Every Day*. See
jkaretnick.com.

"I Commiserate with the Pygmy Octopus Found in the Miami
Beach Parking Garage" was first published in *Michigan Quarterly
Review*.

Douglas Kearney is a Foundation for Contemporary Arts Cy
Twombly awardee and Cave Canem fellow. He is a Griffin Poetry
Prize and Minnesota Book Award winner and a National Book
Award, Pen America, and Kingsley Tufts Award finalist. He has
had four operas staged, most recently *Sweet Land*, which received
rave reviews and was named Opera of the Year (2021) by the
Music Critics Association of North America. He's published
eight books and teaches Creative Writing at the University of
Minnesota–Twin Cities.

Donika Kelly is the author of *The Renunciations* and *Bestiary*. A
recipient of a fellowship from the National Endowment for the
Arts, she is a Cave Canem graduate fellow and founding member
of the collective Poets at the End of the World. She currently
lives in Iowa City, where she teaches creative writing at the
University of Iowa.

"A Poem to Remind Myself of the Natural Order of Things" first
appeared in *The Arkansas International*.

Richard Kenney teaches at the University of Washington. His
most recent book is *Terminator* (Knopf, 2019).

Rachel Kessler is a writer, cartoonist, and educator in
dᶻidᶻəlalič. She co-founded interactive poetry collaborations

Typing Explosion and Vis-à-Vis Society, and collective Wa Na Wari, a residential reclamation project centering Black art and media in Seattle's Central District. Her illustrations of the PNW urban shore feature in *Cascadia Field Guide.*

When she is not swimming with cephalopods, **Sarah Key** feels most at home in a poem, choosing to "dwell in possibility." It is her privilege to dig into words with students and tutors at a community college in the South Bronx where she is Poet-in-Practice. Her poems have been published in such places as *The Georgia Review, Tuesday; An Art Project, Calyx, Poet Lore*, and *Nasty Women Poets.*

Kathleen Kimball-Baker is a writer and editor in Minneapolis, Minnesota. Her poems are (forthcoming) in *Nimrod* and published in *Welter, Blue Mountain Review, Lines + Stars*, and other journals.

Tara King is a writer and choreographer in Albuquerque, NM. King has published poetry and short fiction in *DASH Literary Journal, Avatar Review, Jersey Devil Press*, and others, and has performed internationally. In 2005, she co-founded the award-winning choreographic collective Mad King Thomas. tara-king. com

Susan Landgraf has had more than 400 poems published in *Prairie Schooner, Poet Lore, Margie, Nimrod, Rattle*, and others. Awarded an Academy of American Poets' Laureate award in 2020, her books include *Crossings* in *Triple No. 17* from Ravenna Press Triple Series in 2022, *The Inspired Poet* from Two Sylvias Press, and *What We Bury Changes the Ground* from Tebot Bach. She served as Auburn, Washington's Poet Laureate from 2018-2020.

Katherine Larson's books include *Radial Symmetry*, winner of the Yale Younger Poets Prize; *The Speechless Ones*, winner of the Vercelli International Civic Poetry Prize; and *Wedding of the Foxes,* forthcoming from Milkweed Editions. Her favorite cephalopod is the striped pyjama squid, which is actually a cuttlefish.

"Love at Thirty-Two Degrees" first appeared in *Poetry*.

Seattle writer-artist **David Lasky** co-authored the graphic novel *Carter Family: Don't Forget This Song*, which won comics' Eisner Award in 2013. David has been a graphic novel instructor for over 15 years, and has focused primarily on teaching haiku comics for the past two years.

Irene Latham is a grateful creator of many novels, poetry collections, and picture books, including *Love, Agnes: Postcards from an Octopus* (Lerner, 2018). She lives on a lake in rural Alabama. Visit irenelatham.com to read hundreds of free poems.

Brett Fletcher Lauer is the author of the memoir *Fake Missed Connections: Divorce, Online Dating, and Other Failures* (Soft Skull, 2016) and *A Hotel in Belgium* (Four Way Books, 2014). Lauer is the deputy director of the Poetry Society of America and the poetry editor of *A Public Space*. He lives in New York City.

Emily Lawson is a poet and PhD student in philosophy at the University of British Columbia. As a former Poe/Faulkner Fellow in poetry at the University of Virginia, she taught poetry and served as editor for *Meridian*. Her poems and lyric essays appear or are forthcoming in *Sixth Finch, Adroit, Indiana Review, Waxwing, Thrush, Muzzle, DIAGRAM, BOAAT*, and elsewhere. Her pushcart-nominated fiction appears in *Booth*. She is a stage-III colon cancer survivor.

Donna J. Gelagotis Lee is the author of two award-winning collections, *Intersection on Neptune* (The Poetry Press of Press Americana, 2019), winner of Prize Americana, and *On the Altar of Greece* (Gival Press, 2006), winner of the Gival Press Poetry Award. Her poetry has appeared in numerous journals, including *The Bitter Oleander, Feminist Studies, The Massachusetts Review, Southern Humanities Review, Terrain.org: A Journal of the Built & Natural Environments,* and *Women's Studies Quarterly.*

Jill Leininger is the author of two poetry chapbooks: *Sky Never Sleeps* and *Roof Picnic Skies.* Although this her first publication of poetry since the birth of her child 5 years ago, previous work has been included in *Harvard Review Online, Circumference, Cream City Review,* and *Poetry International.*

Priscilla Long is a Seattle-based writer of poetry, fiction, history, science, and memoir, and a longtime independent teacher of writing. She is author of seven books, the latest being a book on thriving while aging, *Dancing with the Muse in Old Age.* Her books of poems are *Holy Magic* (MoonPath Press) and *Crossing Over: Poems* (University of New Mexico Press).

"Tarot Spread: Divination" first appeared in *Holy Magic* (MoonPath Press).

Oscar Lortz wrote "Cuttlefish (A Sonnet)" when she was seven years old for a contest hosted by Seattle's Cephalopod Appreciation Society. She wanted to write about cuttlefish using "science facts [she] already [knew]." She won an octopus stuffie and eight octopus arms and performed her sonnet at the Hugo House. Oscar currently lives in Kensington, California, and attends Longfellow Middle School in Berkeley.

Pat Lowther headed the League of Canadian Poets and was president of the Writers' Union of Canada before her life was cut short at forty. Her books were and are a triumph over the obstacles of poverty and sexism. She had a passionate sense of justice and a brilliant, loving mind.

"Octopus" was originally published in *A Stone Diary* (Oxford University Press: Toronto, 1977), and later appeared in *Time*

Capsule (Polestar Book Publishers, 1996), and *The Collected Works of Pat Lowther* (NeWest Press, 2010).

Julie Maclean has published seven poetry collections. *When I Saw Jimi* (Indigo Dreams, UK, 2013) was shortlisted for the Crashaw Prize, (Salt, UK). She was joint winner of the inaugural the Geoff Stevens Memorial Poetry Prize. Her work appears in *Poetry* (Chicago), *The Best Australian Poetry* among other international journals. juliemacleanwriter.com

"Emily Dickinson as an Octopus with a Pre-Death Plan" previously appeared in *Cordite Poetry Review.*

Kika Man 文詠玲 (she/they) is a writer from Belgium and Hong Kong. They emphasize tenderness and platonic affections above all. Kika is part of Slam-T, the author of *Let the Mourning Come* (2022), and a PhD Student in Cultural Studies at CUHK. You can find Kika @kikawinling (Twitter/Instagram).

Kindra McDonald is the author of the collections *Fossils* and *In the Meat Years* and was the recipient of the 2020 Haunted Waters Press Poetry Award. She received her MFA from Queens University of Charlotte and is an Adjunct Professor of Writing and Teaching Artist at The Muse Writers Center. She serves as the Poetry Society of Virginia Southeastern region Vice President and you can find her at www.kindramcdonald.com.

Linda Mitchell is a family girl and a Teacher Librarian who writes on the side. Poetry is her first reading and writing love. She makes her way through the kelp fields of a middle school in Northern Virginia.

"haiku Found in *A Handbook to the National Museum* 1886" source material came from "Engravings of Helmet Shell; Mollusks; Calamary; Octopus Swimming & Octopus Crawling." Smithsonian Institution.

"Middle School Octopus" source material came from Alice
Orszulok, "Octopus Focus on Key Features for Camouflage,"
Science Illustrated, 31 May 2012.

Ruth Mota lives in the Santa Cruz Mountains of California
and descends to the sea or to the Monterey Bay Aquarium to
watch the octopus dance whenever possible. Besides writing
poetry she also enjoys facilitating poetry circles to groups in
her community like veterans and men in jail. Her poems have
been published in many online and print journals including:
Terrapin Books, Passager Books, *Gyroscope Review, Tiny Seed
Literary Journal, Canary Literary Journal, Hare's Paw,* and others.

Shankar Narayan explores identity, power, mythology, and
technology in a world where the body is flung across borders
yet possesses unrivaled power to transcend them. Shankar is a
five-time Pushcart Prize nominee and the winner of prizes and
fellowships from Kundiman, Hugo House, Jack Straw, *Flyway,*
4Culture, and *River Heron,* and his chapbook *Postcards From the
New World* won the Paper Nautilus Debut Series chapbook prize.

"Love Letter from Immigrant to Octopus" was previously
published in *Cascadia Field Guide: Art, Ecology, Poetry.*

Jane Wandel Nelson has a lifelong connection to the
waterways of Washington, growing up on Grays Harbor and
spending at least a part of 82 summers on Hood Canal.

"Being the Cuttlefish" previously appeared in *Secrets of the Sea,*
an art and poetry exhibit with an accompanying chapbook at
Lewiston College in Maine (2014).

Sierra Nelson is an award-winning poet, performance
artist, MacDowell Fellow, and founding president of Seattle's
Cephalopod Appreciation Society. She has taught Humanities
courses at University of Washington's Friday Harbor Labs,

and her poems accompanying ichthyologist Dr. Adam Summers' fish skeleton photographs have appeared at the Seattle Aquarium, the Slovenian Natural History Museum, and beyond. Her books include *The Lachrymose Report* (PoetryNW Editions) and collaborative *I Take Back the Sponge Cake* (Rose Metal Press).

"Cephalopod Meditation" debuted as a short film in the Cadence: Video Poetry Festival at NW Film Forum in 2019.

Lesléa Newman has created 80 books for readers of all ages, including the dual memoirs-in-verse, *I Carry My Mother* and *I Wish My Father*; the novel-in-verse, *October Mourning: A Song for Matthew Shepard*; and the children's books, *I Can Be....ME!*, *The Fairest in the Land*, *The Babka Sisters*, *Sparkle Boy*, and *Heather Has Two Mommies*. She has received poetry fellowships from the National Endowment for the Arts and the Massachusetts Artists Foundation. From 2008–2010, she served as the poet laureate of Northampton, MA.

Aimee Nezhukumatathil is the New York Times best-selling author of *Bite by Bite* (food essays), *World of Wonders* (nature essays), and four poetry collections including *Oceanic*. She is professor of English and Creative Writing in the University of Mississippi's MFA program.

"Invitation" appears in *Oceanic* (Copper Canyon Press, 2018).

Katharine Ogle is a poet living in Seattle. Her work has been featured by The Broad Museum in Los Angeles, at a public bus stop in Seattle, in a cocktail menu in San Francisco, and alongside classical composition in Helsinki.

Shin Yu Pai is the Civic Poet of the City of Seattle. Her books include most recently *Virga* (Empty Bowl). Her personal essays have appeared in *Tricycle, YES! Magazine, Seattle Met, Off*

Assignment, and *Zocalo Public Square*. She hosts and produces the *Ten Thousands Things* podcast for KUOW Public Radio/NPR.

"Gyotaku" appeared previously on KUOW's *Seattle Stories*.

Award-winning poet and artist **Pattie Palmer-Baker** creates collages of her poetry using calligraphy and paste paper. She has been nominated for the Pushcart Poetry Prize and published in many journals including *Poeming Pigeons Anthologies, Military Experience & the Arts, Calyx,* and *Phantom Drift*. Her chapbook, *The Color of Goodbye*, was recently published by Kelsay Books, and her book *Five Fundamental Forces* was published by MoonPath Press (2023).

Alixen Pham is a *Best New Poets 2022* finalist and Best of the Net-nominated multidiscipline artist/poet/writer with publications including *The Slowdown featuring Ada Limón, Salamander, Rust+Moth,* and *Apogee Journal*. She leads Women Who Submit's Westside LA chapter, and is the recipient of West Hollywood Artist Grant, Brooklyn Poets Fellowship, and others.

Lisa Usani Phillips is a Massachusetts-based Asian American writer and editor. Her work has appeared in *The Beacon Street Review, Current Biography, House Mountain Review, riksha: Asian American Notes and Images, Salt Magazine,* and *Where the Stories Come From* (edited by Sibyl Johnston, 2000). Honors include the Emerson College Emerging Writer Award for MFA students and the Abrahms Fiction Prize from Connecticut College. lisausaniphillips.com

"Uncommon" was published as part of her debut hybrid collection, *Guest People* (Wheeling Tern Books, 2022).

Based in Vermont, **Verandah Porche** has published *Sudden Eden, The Body's Symmetry,* and *Glancing Off.* She has worked as a writer in residence throughout New England, and composed poems and songs to accompany her community through a generation of moments and milestones.

Rena Priest served as the 6th Washington State Poet Laureate (2021-2023) and was named the 2022 Maxine Cushing Gray Distinguished Writing Fellow by the University of Washington Libraries. She has published two poetry collections and edited two anthologies. She is the recipient of an American Book Award, an Allied Arts Foundation Professional Poets Award, and fellowships from the Academy of American Poets. She holds an MFA from Sarah Lawrence College. Learn more at renapriest.com.

"Shimmy at the Volta" first appeared in *Jack Straw Writers Anthology* vol. 23. A recording of the poem will also appear in the *Soundgarden* installation at the Seattle Conference Center.

A "volta" is a turn at the eighth line in a sonnet. The six lines (sestet) after the volta serve to question or contradict what is addressed in the first eight lines (octave). This poem is written with four octaves and one sestet that answers each of the four octaves.

Cynthia Randolph is an artist and writer who works across photography, video, poetry, and creative nonfiction. Her writing has appeared in journals and anthologies. Her debut poetry collection, *In the Museum of Hunting and Nature,* was published by fmsbw press, June 2023. She lives in San Francisco with her family.

"Labyrinthitis" previously appeared in *In the Museum of Hunting and Nature* (fmsbw press, 2023).

Linda Neal Reising, a Cherokee Nation citizen, has had three Pushcart Prize nominations. *Re-Writing Family History*, was a finalist for the Oklahoma Book Award. *The Keeping*, won the Kops-Fetherling. *Stone Roses* won the Eric Hoffer and Western Heritage; it was also a finalist for the Oklahoma Book Award and WILLA.

"Taking Leave" first appeared in *The Keeping* (Finishing Line Press).

Neil Rhind received his doctorate from Edinburgh University for work on Scottish polymath Alasdair Gray. He has been published in titles including *Eemis Stane, Apricity, The Scottish Literary Review, The International Review of Scottish Studies*, and the *International Journal of Scottish Literature*. He lives in Edinburgh, where he is heavily involved in staging contemporary folk drama.

Kim Roberts is the author of *A Literary Guide to Washington, DC,* and editor of two anthologies of DC poets, most recently *By Broad Potomac's Shore*, selected by the Centers for the Book for the 2021 Route 1 Reads program. Her sixth book of poems, *Corona/Crown*, a cross-disciplinary collaboration with photographer Robert Revere, was published by WordTechEditions (2023). www.kimroberts.org

Gretchen Rockwell is a queer poet whose work has appeared in *AGNI, Cotton Xenomorph, Palette Poetry, Whale Road Review,* and elsewhere; xe has two chapbooks. Gretchen enjoys writing about gender, science, space, and unusual connections. Find xer on Twitter at @daft_rockwell or at www.gretchenrockwell.com.

Matthew Rohrer is the author of ten books of poems, most recently *The Others* which won the Believer Book Award. *Army of Giants* is forthcoming from Wave Books. He lives in Brooklyn.

"Poem for Miroslav Holub" first appeared in *Iterant*.

Kathryn Sadakierski's poems, essays, and reviews have appeared in publications worldwide, including *Critical Read, Literature Today, Miracle Monocle, New Feathers Anthology, Portrait of New England, Publishers Weekly, Silkworm, The Abstract Elephant Magazine, The Curator Magazine,* and *The Parliament Literary Journal*. She holds a B.A. and M.S. from Bay Path University.

Lawrence Schimel is a bilingual (Spanish/English) writer and literary translator, but his only childhood dream was to grow up to be Jacques Cousteau. Severe allergies forced him to give up that dream, and instead study literature. He has now published over 250 books as author or translator. His translations also appear in World Enough Writers' *Ice Cream Poems* and *Coffee Poems* anthologies.

Tina Schumann is the author of *Praising the Paradox, Requiem. A Patrimony of Fugues,* and *As If* as well as editor of *Two-Countries: U.S. Daughters and Sons of Immigrant Parents.* Her work has appeared in *Ascent, Cimarron, Hunger Mountain, Michigan Quarterly, Nimrod, Poetry Daily, Rattle, Verse Daily,* and *The Writer's Almanac.*

Brenda Shaughnessy is the author of seven poetry collections, including *Tanya* (Knopf, 2023), *The Octopus Museum* (a 2019 NYT Notable Book), *Our Andromeda* (finalist for the Griffin International Prize, PEN/Open Book Award, and Kingsley Tufts Prize), and *Human Dark with Sugar* (Academy of American Poets' James Laughlin Award winner and NBCC Award finalist).

"Bakamonotako" was previously published in *The Octopus Museum* (Knopf, 2019).

Ella Shively is a writer and wildlife technician from Wisconsin. Her work has been published in *Runestone Journal, Bracken, Prometheus Dreaming,* and elsewhere. You can find her on Instagram@shivelywrites.

Martha Silano is the author of five books of poetry, most recently *Gravity Assist* (Saturnalia Books, 2019). Her poems have appeared in *Poetry, Paris Review, American Poetry Review,* and *AGNI,* among others. Martha teaches at Bellevue College. marthasilano.net

Pam Yve Simon earned her BA in English and American literature from NYU. Since then, her poetry and photography have been published in ink and pixels. Octopuses have their own ink, and their own "pixels": they change colors as they dream and fascinate Pam. linktr.ee/pamyve

"Wunderpus Photogenicus," in *Olney Magazine*, is an elaboration of "Octopuses Are Known Problem Solvers," here published for the first time.

Derek Smith (opening quote) was born and raised on the Pacific Coast and spent countless hours as a child investigating the shoreline. He now spends counted hours under the surface of the Salish Sea working to inspire the next generation of marine scientists and ocean advocates as a professor at Western Washington University.

Kathryn Smith is a queer poet and mixed-media artist. Her most recent poetry collection, *Self-Portrait with Cephalopod* (Milkweed Editions, 2021), won the Jake Adam York Prize and was a finalist for the 2022 Washington State Book Award. Learn more at kathrynsmithpoetry.com.

"Ode to Super Friends and Nature Television" first appeared in *Self-Portrait with Cephalopod* (Milkweed Editions, 2021).

Sheila Sondik, poet and printmaker, lives in Bellingham, Washington. She loves observing and reading about life forms far removed from human beings. Her poetry has appeared in *CALYX*, *Bracken*, *Pontoon Poetry*, *frogpond*, and elsewhere. Egress Studio Press published her chapbook, *Fishing a Familiar Pond: Found Poetry from The Yearling*, in 2013.

William Stafford was the author of 65 books of poetry, including *The Rescued Year* (1966), *Stories That Could Be True:*

New and Collected Poems (1977), and *An Oregon Message* (1987).
Among his honors and awards were the National Book Award,
the Shelley Memorial Award, the Western States Lifetime
Achievement Award, and a Guggenheim fellowship. In 1970
Stafford was appointed the Poet Laureate to the Library of
Congress, and in 1975 the Poet Laureate of Oregon. He taught at
Lewis and Clark College in Portland, Oregon, from 1948-1980.

"Aquarium at Seaside" is reprinted from *Braided Apart*, by
Kim Stafford & William Stafford (Confluence Press, 1976), by
permission of the Estate of William Stafford.

from Kim Stafford: When William and Dorothy Stafford took their
kids to the Oregon coast, one regular stop was a salty, steamy,
boisterous aquarium in the town of Seaside, where you could
throw a fish to a seal slapping the concrete pool, and watch the
octopus sidle sly and easy from one corner of its tank to the
other. I remember my father leaning close to watch his wild
cousin's gentle dance.

Cecilia Stancell is a lover of words and writing. A life-long
dancer, she holds master's degrees in photography and art
history. She is deeply intrigued by the worlds of legend and
myth and how these live in our minds, memories, and bodies.
She lives in upstate New York.

Based in the PNW, **Jen Strongin** (front and back cover photos)
is a professional photographer, educator and naturalist. She
finds great inspiration in the natural world, both deep in the
wild and on the edges of her urban habitat in Seattle, WA.
Her photography explores the intersections of land and sea,
urban and wild, science and art. She encourages her viewers
to walk alongside her in these spaces, to be transported to
worlds beyond their own for a brief moment in time, to revel
in joy and wonder at the beauty of our home planet. www.
jenstronginphotography.com

Jennifer K. Sweeney is the author of four poetry collections, *Foxlogic, Fireweed; Little Spells;* James Laughlin Award winner *How to Live on Bread and Music;* and *Salt Memory*. Recent awards include a Pushcart Prize, the Terrain Poetry Prize, and the Backwaters Poetry Award. She writes, teaches, and makes literary collages in Redlands, California.

In "Octopus Tango," quotes taken from *Teaching Argentine Tango in New York,* 1914 by Mr. and Mrs. Castle Vernon.

Arianne True (Choctaw, Chickasaw) is a queer poet and teaching artist from Seattle and has spent most of her work time working with youth. She's received fellowships and residencies from Artist Trust and the Seattle Repertory Theater, among others, and is a proud alum of Hedgebrook and of the MFA program at the Institute of American Indian Arts. She lives near the Salish Sea with her cat. Arianne is the 2023-2025 Washington State Poet Laureate.

"Encoded Anatomies" first appeared in The Rumpus's National Poetry Month series (2022).

Emily Tuszynska lives in Virginia, just outside Washington, DC. Her poems have appeared in many journals, most recently including *EcoTheo Review, Terrain.org, Southern Poetry Review,* and *Prairie Schooner.*

Barbara Ungar's sixth book, *After Naming the Animals,* was published by The Word Works (2023). Other poems from this collection have appeared in *Scientific American, Crazyhorse, Comstock Review, Cutthroat, Gargoyle, Hypertext, Pedestal, Atticus Review, Small Orange,* and others. A professor of English at The College of Saint Rose, she lives in Saratoga Springs, New York. www.barbaraungar.net

Hannah Viano is an artist and educator based in Twisp, Washington. "I seek out projects that give me the opportunity to illustrate important ecological stories, challenge me to compellingly depict subjects and ideas, and use education to foster stewardship and a sense of place. This work comes to life through children's books, teaching residencies, science outreach, cross-pollinator expeditions, and community focused public art projects."

O is part of a series of papercut images created for a project funded by the Seattle CityArtist grant which later became the book *S is for Salmon-A Pacific Northwest Alphabet* (Sasquatch Press).

Cody Walker is the author of several poetry collections, including *The Self-Styled No-Child* (Waywiser, 2016). His work appears in *The New York Times Magazine* and two editions of *The Best American Poetry*. He directs the Bear River Writers' Conference in Northern Michigan and lives with his family in Ann Arbor.

"From Sonnet to Stage" originally appeared in *Light Quarterly* in 2009.

JR Walsh is the Online Editor at *The Citron Review*. Born in Syracuse, NY, he now teaches English as a Second Language in Boise, ID. His writing is in beloved publications such as *New World Writing, Litro, Juked, Hobart, HOOT, Rejection Letters, FRiGG, Blink-Ink, B O D Y, The Hong Kong Review, The Greensboro Review,* and *Esquire*. itsjrwalsh.com

Lylium Walsh is an editor and writer based in Edmonds, WA. She has been published in *My Edmonds News* repeatedly and placed second in poetry for EPIC Group Writers' 2021 writing contest. She previously led Writing Rainbow, a meetup for LGBTQIA+ writers. More about her can be found at lyliumwalsh.com.

Michael Waters' books include *Sinnerman* (Etruscan Press, 2023), *Caw* (BOA Editions, 2020), & *The Dean of Discipline* (University of Pittsburgh Press, 2018). His coedited anthologies include *Border Lines: Poems of Migration* (Knopf, 2020). A 2017 Guggenheim Fellow, recipient of five Pushcart Prizes & fellowships from the NEA, Fulbright Foundation, & NJ State Council on the Arts, Waters lives in Ocean, NJ.

Using reference photos, classic scientific and children's illustration, and personal research as touchstones, daughter of Pat Lowther and coloured pencil artist **Beth Wilks** aims to synthesize and reveal the essence of our common ground with nonhuman animals through careful rendering of facial and physical expression unique to each species.

Cassondra Windwalker writes full-time from the southern Alaskan coast. Her latest novel, *Love Like A Cephalopod,* was published in February 2023 by Bayou Wolf Press. She is also the poet of the full-length poetry collections *The Almost-Children* and *tide tables and tea with god,* as well as the Helen Kay Award-winning chapbook *The Bench.*

Catherine Wing is the author of two collections of poetry, *Enter Invisible* and *Gin & Bleach.* Her poems have been published in such journals as *Poetry*, *The Nation*, and *Tin House.* She teaches at Kent State University and with the NEOMFA, the nation's only consortial program in Creative Writing.

Deborah Woodard's most recent poetry collection is *No Finis: Triangle Testimonies, 1911* (Ravenna Press, 2018). Her chapbook *Hunter Mnemonics* (hemel press, 2008) was illustrated by artist Heide Hinrichs. She has translated the poetry of Amelia Rosselli from Italian, most recently in *Obtuse Diary* (Entre Rios Books, 2018), and *The Dragonfly* (Entre Rios Books, 2023). Deborah teaches at Hugo House, a literary center in Seattle.

Susan J. Wurtzburg received the Elizabeth M. Campbell Poetry Award, with semi-finalist status in the Crab Creek Review Poetry and Naugatuck River Review's Narrative Poetry Contests. Her poetry appears in *Bindweed Magazine, Crosswinds Poetry Journal, Poetry and Covid, Rat's Ass Review, The Literary Nest, Verse-Virtual, WayWords,* and *Quince Magazine.*

Jeffrey Yang is the author of poetry collections *Line and Light; Hey, Marfa; Vanishing-Line;* and *An Aquarium,* as well as numerous books of translation. He is also editor of the anthologies *Birds, Beasts, and Seas: Nature Poems,* and *Time of Grief: Mourning Poems,* and the collection *The Sea Is a Continual Miracle: Sea Poems and Other Writings by Walt Whitman.* Yang works as an editor at New Directions Publishing and *New York Review of Books.*

"Octopus" and "Squid" originally appeared in *An Aquarium* (2008) by Jeffrey Yang. Reprinted with the permission of Graywolf Press.

Matthew Zapruder is the author of five collections of poetry, most recently *Father's Day,* as well as *Why Poetry,* and *Story of a Poem.* He is editor at large at Wave Books, where he edits contemporary poetry, prose, and translations. He was the Editor of Best American Poetry 2022, and teaches in the MFA in Creative Writing at Saint Mary's College of California.

Mari Zeng was raised by wolves in the Pacific Northwest. She holds a BFA from the University of Washington. She was trapped in NYC by the quarantine, where she still resides.